Employment Law from Birth to Death

The complementary website

The http://books.indicator.co.uk website gives you instant access to all the ready-to-use documents, tools, policies, etc. that complement this publication.

Go to
http://books.indicator.co.uk

The CD-ROM

Don't have access to the Internet?
Call Customer Services on 01233 653500 to request a CD-ROM.

ISBN 978-1-906892-24-1

First Edition - Third print - E01P3

Introduction

Employment Law from Birth to Death

As an employer you know full well what a thankless task it is to get to grips with employment law. Just think about all those rights your staff have. Fail to fully understand what they are or to have the correct paperwork in place, and your employees will walk all over you, costing a tidy sum along the way.

Employees start to gain protection from the moment they apply for a job. Reject the application incorrectly and you could be on the receiving end of a discrimination claim. And once they join they'll acquire hundreds of rights that you need to stay in control of.

In this book you'll discover all that you need to know about these rights, literally covering everything from birth to death. It starts with the position before appointment, and then covers from day one through the different milestones ending with post-employment rights. It guides you through the employment minefield, clearly showing what you must do to stay on the right side of the law and where there's room to exercise some discretion. Plus, it comes with a stack of ready-to-use documents.

Table of contents

Chapter 1 - Before employment begins

Chapter 2 - From day one

Chapter 3 - First month of employment

Chapter 4 - After eight weeks of employment

Chapter 5 - At six months

Chapter 6 - At one year

Table of contents

Chapter 7 - At two years

Chapter 8 - Post-employment

Chapter 9 - Documents

CHAPTER 1

Before employment begins

Some individuals enjoy employment protection before they've even been offered a job. These all relate to discrimination, and the groups can be divided into two main categories. The first include those who are protected because of a particular characteristic and the second are those protected due to their affiliation, or lack thereof, with a trade union. So what claims can they bring?

1.1. DISCRIMINATION

1.1.1. Type of discrimination claim

Discrimination on the grounds of:

- age
- sex
- race
- disability
- sexual orientation
- gender reassignment
- religion or belief.

What is the risk?

Unlimited compensation.

How does it work?

During the last decade, the number of groups protected by discrimination legislation has grown considerably. As a result, a job applicant can mount a claim against you if they believe that they were rejected on one or more of the seven grounds listed above. It's important to remember that they only have to enquire about a vacancy: they don't even need to be offered the job. This follows a finding by the European Court of Justice (ECJ) in 2008.

In that case, a Belgian company had used a job ad which stated that it wouldn't employ immigrants because its clients *"don't like dealing with them"*. The ECJ found that the wording it used amounted to direct discrimination on the grounds of race. Prior to this case, only the Equality and Human Rights Commission could bring claims on behalf of an individual but this case threw open the tribunal doors to those who seek to bring claims.

At present, age discrimination is the most popular type of claim. It also seems to be the hardest for employers to get to grips with. This is partly because it's quite new - entering the statute books on October 1 2006 - but also because society itself is inherently ageist. Many words have become associated with a particular age group. For example, ads targeting older workers tend to focus on the type of person required, e.g. "mature" or someone with "ten years' relevant experience"; employers wanting young workers have tended to emphasise the nature of the working environment, describing it as being "young and dynamic", "lively" and "fast paced".

Specifying certain qualifications, such as GCSEs, which have only existed for around the last 20 years, can also cause problems. Their inclusion without the accompanying words "or equivalent qualifications" gives the impression that a much younger age group is being targeted. Unfortunately, if you use this type of phrase but then either don't interview a particular candidate, or reject them following an interview, you could face an age discrimination claim.

Note. As there's no requirement for an individual to be an employee and the potential compensatory award is unlimited, alleging some form of discrimination at the recruitment stage has become increasingly popular. As a result, some individuals have made it their career to apply for a variety of jobs and then sue employers for discrimination.

One example of this dubious practice concerns the case of Margaret Keane, a 51 year-old chartered accountant with 18 years' post-qualification experience. She successfully made over £120,000 by claiming that her job applications for newly qualified/entry-level positions were rejected solely because of her age. She managed to accuse 22 companies of "ageism" of which twelve agreed to out-of-court settlements, earning her at least £10,000 each time. Luckily, a tribunal has now rejected five more claims after the latest companies she tried it on with fought back. It also ruled that an applicant must have a genuine desire to do the job applied for, i.e. they can't bring a claim if they had no intention of ever doing the work.

Examples of potentially discriminatory ads are given below:

Age:

"We require a dynamic school leaver who wants to build a career in a lively and fast-paced environment."

"This vacancy would suit someone looking for their first job."

"Our desired applicant will be mature, educated to post graduate level in a relevant subject and will have ten years' work experience."

Disability:

"All applicants must be physically fit and able to carry out heavy-lifting duties when required."

"This position requires lots of walking, and won't be suitable for a disabled person."

Sex:

"We have a vacancy for an odd job man."

"Due to the nature of our working environment, a male applicant is preferred."

"We have a part-time vacancy which is ideal for young mothers."

"As this job involves extensive travel, it's only suitable for those who don't have family commitments."

Sexual orientation:

"Due to company values, gay applicants should not apply."

Religion and belief:

"Female employees will be expected to wear a uniform consisting of a skirt suit."

"BNP supporters need not apply."

How to avoid it?

Always ensure that you use non-discriminatory phrases in job ads for example.

"We are looking for someone who wishes to build a career within our company."

"Our desired applicant will be an experienced engineer with particular knowledge of…"

"We are looking for someone with five GCSEs or equivalent qualifications."

"We have a vacancy for a handyman/woman."

"This role involves some travel to other sites/abroad."

"Ethnic minorities and the disabled are currently under-represented in our business and are particularly welcome to apply."

Also, be aware that indirect discrimination will arise if you seek to impose a particular requirement (or in legal terms, a provision, criterion or practice) that may disadvantage a particular group unnecessarily; for example, unreasonably insisting that all applicants are UK citizens, or by setting a minimum height requirement for a job. This would unfairly disadvantage women as they tend to be shorter than men, and far fewer women could apply as a result.

EMPLOYER TIP

If you use a recruitment agency, they should help you draft the ad as part of their service, but do double check that any ads they use don't accidentally discriminate in any way.

There are a couple of documents which will help to ensure that you don't discriminate during the recruitment process. The first is a well-drafted recruitment policy that sets out the steps that you will follow during the process. The second is a job description and person specification that will help you identify and focus on the skills and experience that you require.

Download Zone

For a **Recruitment Policy**, visit **http://books.indicator.co.uk**. You'll find the access code on page 2 of this book.

Download Zone

For a **Job Description and Person Specification**, visit **http://books.indicator. co.uk**. You'll find the access code on page 2 of this book.

1.2.   TRADE UNION MEMBERSHIP

1.2.1.   Risks regarding trade union membership

There may be a claim for refusing employment because an individual is, or is not, a trade union member.

What is the risk?

Maximum compensation of £65,300.

For this type of claim, the level of compensation is the same as the compensatory award for unfair dismissal. It exists by virtue of s.137(1)(a) of the **Trade Union and Labour Relations (Consolidation) Act 1992** (TULRCA). As a result, any job applicant who believes that they were rejected for employment by you (or an employment agency) on the basis that they are, or are not, a member of a trade union, can mount a tribunal claim.

How does it work?

This new right was introduced because a job applicant can't claim for unfair dismissal (this relies on the individual being employed). However, a claim under TULRCA will work in the exactly the same way. According to the government's Business, Innovation and Skills website, refusal of employment will be deemed to involve one (or more) of the following:

- refusing or deliberately omitting to deal with an application or enquiry
- causing the job applicant to withdraw or to stop pursuing an application or enquiry, e.g. by making threats or discouraging remarks
- refusing or deliberately omitting to offer employment of the kind being sought
- making an offer of employment of the kind being sought but on terms, e.g. the rate of pay, that no reasonable employer who wished to fill the vacancy would offer, and which isn't accepted, or
- making an offer of employment of the kind sought but withdrawing it or causing it not to be accepted, e.g. by making threats or discouraging remarks.

Where a tribunal finds that a claimant was refused employment on this ground it can: **(1)** make a declaration that the individual was unlawfully refused employment, or the services of an employment agency; **(2)** require the prospective employer, and/or the employment agency, to pay compensation; and **(3)** recommend that the claimant is considered for a job.

Risk. In the event that the tribunal upholds a claim and recommends that you take certain action, e.g. to employ the claimant and you fail to comply, it can increase the amount of any compensatory award made (providing that you lack reasonable justification for failing to comply).

How to avoid it?

This type of claim is easily avoided by not asking job applicants at interview whether or not they are union members. Equally, if you use an application form during your recruitment process, don't ask applicants if they are a union member (unless your organisation is a trade union).

EMPLOYER TIP

If you employ 20 or fewer workers, you can't be forced by law to recognise a trade union in your workplace.

Download Zone

For an **Application Form**, visit **http://books.indicator.co.uk**. You'll find the access code on page 2 of this book.

1.2.2.   Blacklisting of a job applicant

There may be a claim if a job applicant is blacklisted on the grounds of trade union membership or activism.

What's the risk?

Minimum compensatory award of £5,000 and up to £65,300 in an employment tribunal.

An injunction can be issued by a civil court to prevent the use of a blacklist and it can also award unlimited compensation.

On March 2 2010 the **Employment Relations Act 1999 (Blacklisting) Regulations 2010** were introduced. They outlaw the compilation, distribution and use of blacklists that contain details of trade union members and activists by employers and employment agencies. The amount of compensation awarded to an individual will depend on the loss suffered. In some cases, there may also be a sum awarded for injury to feelings (subject to the maximum limit). In addition, there could be sanctions under the **Data Protection Act 1998** because the individual hasn't given consent to their details being held.

How does it work?

Blacklisting describes the creation of a list of individuals that organisations are advised not to employ, usually on the grounds of trade union membership or activism. In 2009, it was found that 44 employers in the construction industry had paid an organisation called "The Consulting Association" (TCA) for access to a blacklist of 3,000 names. For £3,000 a year, or £2.20 for each individual's details, these construction companies were able to weed out trade union members and/or activists from descriptions such as, *"lazy and a trouble stirrer"* and *"ex-shop steward definite problems - no go"*. In order to combat this (and to appease the unions), the Regulations render the following practices unlawful:

- to compile, supply, sell or use a "prohibited list"
- to refuse employment to a job applicant for a reason related to a "prohibited list"
- for an employment agency to refuse to provide its services to an individual, e.g. to put them forward for jobs, for a reason related to a "prohibited list".

Note. It's also illegal to dismiss an employee or subject them to any other detriment, e.g. victimisation, for a reason connected to a "prohibited list".

How to avoid it?

In order to avoid problems, don't access information from a "prohibited list". To qualify as such a list, it must: **(1)** contain details of individuals who are trade union members or who have taken (or are taking part) in trade union activities; and **(2)** have been created with a view to employers or employment agencies using it to discriminate against certain job applicants during the recruitment process. Under these new Regulations, the onus will be on you as an employer to convince a tribunal that you haven't breached them. This is because they will adopt the principle of reverse burden of proof. In practice, this means that if a job applicant can show that their name was on a prohibited list and that they were refused employment despite possessing suitable qualifications and/or experience, the tribunal must conclude that the failure to employ was connected to the blacklist. It will then be down to the employer to show that the rejection was for a completely unconnected reason.

KEY POINTS

Job applicants are legally protected from discrimination on the grounds of:

- age
- sex
- race
- disability
- sexual orientation
- gender re-assignment
- religion or religious belief; and
- being a trade union member or activist (or not if it is required).

Pre-employment discrimination can result in the following penalties:

- unlimited compensation for discrimination on the grounds of age, sex, race, disability, sexual orientation, gender re-assignment, religion or religious belief
- up to £65,300 in a tribunal for refusing employment because of union membership (or lack of)
- between £5,000 - £65,300 at tribunal for blacklisting an applicant on the grounds of trade union membership/activism
- in a civil court, an injunction may be issued to prevent you from using a blacklist
- unlimited compensation if the case is brought in a civil court.

You can avoid such claims by:

- using a carefully drafted recruitment policy
- identifying the skills and experience you need with a job description and person specification
- ensuring that you don't ask about trade union membership on your application form
- not accessing details of individuals held on prohibited "blacklists".

CHAPTER 2

From day one

From the very first day of employment your employees will have numerous rights. They don't earn them after a qualifying period, and this often catches employers unaware. These rights cover a wide range of areas but they can broadly be divided into the following groups: **(1)** contractual entitlements; **(2)** the right to privacy **(3)** automatic protection against unfair dismissal in clearly defined circumstances; **(4)** pay; **(5)** parent/family friendly; **(6)** discipline and grievance; **(7)** health and safety; and **(8)** time off (in certain circumstances).

2.1. CONTRACTUAL ISSUES

2.1.1. Breach of contract

What's the risk?

£25,000 maximum award for breach of contract claims heard at tribunal.

Unlimited compensation for a claim brought in a county court or the High Court.

Note. For this type of claim to be brought at tribunal (and so for the £25,000 compensation cap to apply), it must arise on, or be outstanding at, the point of the termination of employment. But it can't relate to any term that: **(1)** is a restrictive covenant; **(2)** relates to intellectual property rights, e.g. copyright and patents; or **(3)** imposes an obligation of confidence; neither can the dispute relate to personal injury (these are dealt with outside of employment proceedings). For county court and High Court claims and those where a tribunal has jurisdiction, the risk generally lies in making too many terms contractual. This increases the potential for conflict, as the number of terms that you can't vary unilaterally is that much greater. Another risky area is inadequate consultation over any contractual changes that you wish or, indeed, need to make, or a failure to undertake them altogether.

> **EMPLOYER TIP**
>
> Continuous employment starts on the very first day in the job. It can't be deferred to a later point, e.g. following the satisfactory completion of probation.

How does it work?

An employment contract is a legally binding agreement that exists between you and an employee. It will primarily consist of written, or express, terms that describe how the relationship will operate. For example, it will cover remuneration, working hours and holiday entitlement. However, it will also include implied terms that are treated as being part of every contract, even though they are not actually written into it. These include the "duty of trust and confidence" as well as an employee's duty to obey all reasonable instructions given. A "breach of contract" will occur when either party breaks one (or more) of these terms; be it express, implied or one that has been subject to mutual verbal agreement. If you don't have an employee's express agreement to a contractual change, they may work under the new terms and conditions under protest. Should this happen, you would still be in breach of contract as they have not accepted the terms. But there's a limit on the amount of time that an employee can continue to do this and keep open the option of resigning and claiming constructive dismissal. Each case will turn on its own facts and circumstances.

In terms of tactics, whilst an employee or legal representative may be tempted to embellish a claim in order to get it into a county court, the good news is that damages are only awarded for any financial loss suffered.

EMPLOYER TIP

An employee can't instigate a claim in a tribunal and then switch it over to a civil court in order to re-litigate the same complaint and sue for the difference. They only get one bite at the cherry.

Note. If the position was reversed and an employee breaches their contract (and it's financially viable for you to pursue them for damages), you would normally use a county court. You could only use a tribunal if your action is in response to a breach of contract claim already made against you by an employee, i.e. a counter-claim.

How to avoid it?

You can't make unilateral changes to contracts and ask staff to agree without any consultation (basic contractual principles mean that both parties need to agree). So you need to: **(1)** notify employees of the contractual change(s) that you propose to make; **(2)** explain what business reasons lie behind it; **(3)** have a genuine two-way consultation with staff over any concerns that they may have; and **(4)** obtain their written agreement. If you avoid, or only pay lip service to, this process, there's a risk that they will resign and claim breach of contract and/or constructive dismissal.

Where you find yourself needing to make contractual changes, always work through the following steps:

Step 1. Reasons. Before you notify employees, be sure that you are not only clear on the changes that you propose to make, e.g. to notice periods or working hours, but that you can clearly show the business benefits, i.e. they are justified.

Step 2. Consultation. Consult with staff and listen to any concerns that they may have. It may be that they have alternative ideas you haven't considered; be prepared to incorporate them into any planned changes that you wish to make. You're also likely to have an easier time if you refer to your desired changes as "proposals" rather than as something that will be introduced no matter what employees think.

Step 3. Incentives. Agreement may be more quickly reached if you offer staff a financial "sweetener" to agree to the new changes, such as a one-off loyalty bonus. But if you're thinking of offering more permanent benefits as an incentive, e.g. extra leave or a pay rise, work out the financial implications properly first.

Step 4. New contracts. Once you've secured agreement to the changes, give them at least three months' notice (ideally longer) of the changes before issuing new contracts.

Step 5. Dealing with dissenters. Should one or more employees refuse to accept the changes, simply issue them with new contracts and inform them of the date that they will become effective. Also, make it clear that if they still won't accept the terms, their employment will end when the new contract takes effect. If, having done this, they continue to work without protest, you are entitled to assume from their conduct that they've accepted the new terms.

You can reduce the likelihood of a breach of contract claim by incorporating flexible clauses into your employment contracts where appropriate. This will allow you some room to manoeuvre, providing that any proposed alteration is reasonable. Common examples include:

- **Bonus payments.** Many breach of contract cases that reach tribunals and the courts (particularly the High Court) are over bonus payments. They tend to arise when an employee alleges that the non-payment of a bonus is a breach of contract. Luckily, this risk can be greatly reduced by retaining the right to keep any payment of bonuses discretionary, i.e. down to you. Providing you exercise such discretion fairly and consistently, in other words you treat all employees equally, you will be safe. This can be done via the use of a bonus payment clause.

Download Zone

For a **Bonus Payment Clause**, visit **http://books.indicator.co.uk**. You'll find the access code on page 2 of this book.

© EMPLOYMENT LAW FROM BIRTH TO DEATH, Indicator

From day one

2

- **Flexibility.** On occasion, you may need staff to put in extra hours to get the job done, particularly in the event of an emergency, or unforeseen circumstances that could impact on your business. With this in mind, you could insert a flexibility clause into your contracts that states employees may be required to work such *"additional hours as are reasonably necessary in order to carry out their duties effectively"*. However, this must be reasonable, and staff can't be expected to work excessively. It also can't be used to get around the 48-hour maximum week imposed by the **Working Time Directive 1998**.

Download Zone

For a **Flexibility Clause**, visit **http://books.indicator.co.uk**. You'll find the access code on page 2 of this book.

- **Job flexibility.** In order to save on the costs of recruiting new staff, or having to pay for agency temps, you could usefully retain a flexible job duties clause in your contracts. This allows you to require an employee to perform a task or assume a responsibility that isn't detailed in their job description. However, you must be mindful of the implied duty of trust and confidence. In this context, it will mean not expecting the employee to carry out tasks that are beyond their level of capability and experience, or those that could be considered to be demeaning in some way. For example, asking your office manager to clean the toilets.

Download Zone

For a **Flexible Job Duties Clause**, visit **http://books.indicator.co.uk**. You'll find the access code on page 2 of this book.

- **Mobility.** Another area where a flexible job clause is advantageous is where you may need to transfer an employee to another site. This could be close to their current workplace, or in another part of the country. Yet in order to do this safely you need to have an express mobility and relocation clause in your contracts, as tribunals will only allow you to imply very restricted terms. So if you want the flexibility to move an employee further afield, you must first retain the specific contractual right to do so. With careful drafting, you will be able to do this on a temporary as well as a permanent basis.

Download Zone

For a **Mobility and Relocation Clause**, visit **http://books.indicator.co.uk**. You'll find the access code on page 2 of this book.

As a general point, you can also reduce the likelihood of a breach of contract claim by keeping as many benefits as possible on a non-contractual footing. This will allow you to make unilateral changes as and when necessary, although we would advise you to explain to staff why this is happening first. Whilst it's not exhaustive, the following areas are those that you are likely to want to update more frequently and could also take the form of policies instead of contractual clauses:

1. **Expenses.** You may need to alter the type of expenses that you allow employees to reclaim and/or the amount. Equally, you may need to make changes with regards to the circumstances where you allow employees to reclaim their expenses.

Download Zone

For a **Reimbursement of Expenses Policy**, visit **http://books.indicator.co.uk**. You'll find the access code on page 2 of this book.

2. **Sickness absence.** If you have a sickness absence problem, e.g. with one-day sickies, you may wish to revise your company sick pay scheme. For example, reducing the amount of money that you pay for each day absent from full pay to 60% of salary or less.

Download Zone.

For a **Sickness Absence Policy**, visit **http://books.indicator.co.uk**. You'll find the access code on page 2 of this book.

3. **Training.** If you pay for staff training, you may wish to amend your policy on how funding operates. It may be that you want to extend the period in which any clawback of training costs can be recouped, e.g. from one year to two, or amend your rules for allowing time off to re-sit an exam.

Note. The new right to request time off for training was introduced on April 6 2010 but it currently only applies to organisations with 250 or more staff. It will be extended to cover all other employers on April 6 2011.

Download Zone

For a **Training and Development Policy**, visit **http://books.indicator.co.uk**. You'll find the access code on page 2 of this book.

2.1.2. No less favourable treatment of part-time employees

What's the risk?

Unlimited compensation.

How does it work?

There's no legal definition of a part-time worker but it's taken to mean someone who works for less than 35 hours per week. The rights of part-time workers are protected by the **Part-time Workers (Prevention of Less Favourable Treatment) Regulations 2000**. As their name suggests, these Regulations ensure that part-time workers receive the same treatment (on a pro rata basis) as an employee working full-time hours. This not only refers to pay and benefits but also access to training and promotion opportunities. A part-timer can only be treated less favourably if there's "objective justification" for doing so. In layman's terms this means that you have to show the reason for different treatment is necessary in order to meet a genuine business aim. For example, you can't deny them a bonus payment because they are part-time. However, what you can do is pay it pro rata. So if you operate a 40-hour week and a part-time employee works 20 hours, you can pay them half the bonus that they would have accrued had they worked full-time.

Since the case of **Matthews and Others v Kent & Medway Towns and Fire Authority 2006**, it has become harder to justify different treatment of part-time workers. This is because the ruling prevented employers from arguing that if part-timers were employed on: **(1)** different types of contract and; **(2)** not doing the "same or broadly similar work", they could be denied equal treatment. Instead, it's now the position that if both groups are employed under a contract of employment, then it's deemed to be the same.

When looking at whether the same or broadly similar work is being undertaken, the issue isn't whether the work is different but if it's similar. This means that a tribunal will look first for the similarities between the work carried out by a full-time employee and their part-time equivalent. As a result, you can no longer justify unequal treatment simply on the basis that full-time employees do extra tasks.

How to avoid it?

You can do much to reduce the likelihood of a claim by remembering the following points:

- **Pay.** You must pay part-time staff the same hourly rate that you would a full-timer carrying out a similar job. However, if you pay overtime, you can require part-time staff to work the same number of hours as a full-time employee before the right to earn overtime payments is triggered, e.g. 40 hours per week.

- **Occupational pension schemes.** Part-time workers should have equal access to any occupational pension scheme that you operate, albeit on a pro rata basis.

- **Benefits.** Equally, you need to review your benefits package to ensure that part-time employees are not denied access. As with pension schemes, access can be on a pro rata basis unless it's not practical to do so, such as offering discounted gym membership.

- **Training and career development.** Periodically, check that part-time employees are not being excluded from training opportunities etc. In terms of timing of courses, you should not experience problems if you hold training courses at a time that will suit most employees, including part-timers.

- **Holidays.** The statutory annual leave entitlement for full-time staff is 5.6 weeks (28 days including the eight bank and public holidays). For part-time staff, you simply calculate their statutory leave entitlement on a pro rata basis.

Example

Employee works four days a week. So:

Number of days worked ÷ days in working week × annual holiday entitlement = employee leave.

4 ÷ 5 x 28 = 22.4 days' leave entitlement.

EMPLOYER TIP

If this equation produces a fraction (as with our example), you can't round down the number of days given, as this would be unfavourable treatment. Instead, you should convert the fractions into hours.

If you give your full-time employees a more generous leave entitlement than that provided for by working time legislation, e.g. 5.6 weeks plus the eight bank and public days, you must offer the same to part-time staff but again on a pro rata basis.

EMPLOYER TIP

You can require part-time staff to take bank holidays when they coincide with their working days.

Another area that can cause problems is the allocation of leave with respect to bank and public holidays. This tends to arise most frequently with those whose working days include Mondays and Fridays; they are immediately guaranteed five of the eight days off, i.e. four bank holiday Mondays plus Good Friday. If you factor in the possibility of Christmas Day, Boxing Day and New Year's Day falling on either a Monday or Friday, then these part-timers are laughing. If, on the other hand, you have some part-timers who work Tuesdays, Wednesdays and Thursdays, they will lose out.

Luckily, there's an easy solution to this problem: simply work out bank and public holiday entitlement on a pro rata basis.

Example

Employee works four days a week. So:

Number of days worked ÷ days in working week x annual bank holidays = employee's entitlement.

4 ÷ 5 x 8 = 6.4 days' bank and public holiday entitlement.

In our example, this could then be rounded up to 6.5 bank holidays which can be taken by mutual agreement. This way nobody will feel that others are profiting unfairly simply because they work on different days.

2.1.3.   No less favourable treatment of fixed-term contract employees

What's the risk?

Unlimited compensation.

How does it work?

Fixed-term contracts are attractive to employers as they allow you to recruit staff to work on specific projects (known as a "specific task contracts") without having to increase your headcount permanently. Equally, they allow you to recruit for a defined time period, such as a six-month contract with a specified end date, e.g. to cover maternity leave. Unfortunately, this type of contract isn't as attractive as it used to be due to the **Fixed-term Employees (Prevention of Less Favourable Treatment) Regulations 2002**.

This is for two main reasons. Firstly, the protection afforded to those working on fixed-term contracts has increased, particularly those working on specific task contracts. This is because previously, once a specific task contract came to an end it wasn't treated as a dismissal, and so the employee had no legal protection under dismissal law. This was in contrast to other fixed-term contracts that were scheduled to end on a pre-determined date, where those working under them were protected by dismissal law. These Regulations have now ensured a level playing field, so that when any fixed-term contract ends it will count as a dismissal. This means that anyone engaged for a fixed-term contract that lasts twelve months or more can potentially claim unfair dismissal; it isn't possible to ask an employee to waive their rights under these Regulations.

Secondly, you can't now employ employees on a fixed-term contract that grants them inferior terms to your permanent staff. This applies to remuneration (including

---

pensions), holidays, pay, opportunities for training, contractual terms and the opportunity to obtain permanent employment with you, e.g. you can't exclude fixed-term employees from applying for posts advertised internally. Some unwary employers still don't understand this and have ended up in tribunal as a result.

Note. Should an employee believe that they are being treated less favourably than their permanent counterparts, they can write to you and ask why this is. You are required to respond in writing within 21 days.

Another problem will arise if you recruit an employee on a fixed-term contract and then need to terminate it early. This could be because you discover that they are not up to the job in some way or that, due to unforeseen circumstances, you must end the contract earlier than expected. If you don't make provision for this, you could be landed with a breach of contract claim.

How to avoid it?

With regards to less favourable treatment of fixed-term employees, your defence is that of "objective justification". This requires you to show that different treatment is necessary and appropriate in order to allow you to achieve a legitimate and genuine business objective. For example, it may not be cost-effective for you to offer pro-rata benefits to those on fairly short fixed-term contracts, such as company loans. Alternatively, you could argue that the value of the fixed-term employee's terms and conditions are at least equal to those of comparable permanent staff, assuming, of course, that they are.

EMPLOYER TIP

If a fixed-term employee is expected to work for you for less than one year, look at offering benefits such as health insurance or staff discounts pro rata.

Another area where you could fall foul of the law is with pension contributions. Avoid this by offering fixed-term employees access to any occupational pension scheme you operate on the same basis that you would for permanent employees. However, you don't have to offer special alternative benefits, such as contributions to a private pension scheme to those who don't elect to join a pension scheme, unless you offer it to comparable permanent employees.

Finally, you can retain the right to terminate a fixed-term contract early. This can be done by incorporating an early termination clause into your fixed-term contracts. It should state that early termination may happen should circumstances outside your control occur and what notice period will be given.

Example

"Your appointment is on a fixed-term basis. Whilst your contract is expected to continue until ...... (insert date), unforeseen circumstances that are outside the Company's control may mean that notice has to be given before the contract is due to terminate. In the unlikely event that this occurs, your contract can be terminated by the giving of ...... (insert notice period). Should this happen, you will be paid your salary and benefits up until the new effective termination date."

If you don't do this and attempt to unilaterally terminate the contract, you could find yourself on the receiving end of a tribunal claim for breach of contract. This could work out to be expensive (and time-consuming) because you may end up having to pay the employee a sum equal to their net pay for the unexpired portion of the contract. Plus, you would also be liable to compensate them for any benefits lost during this period, such as medical insurance.

KEY POINTS

New employees are protected from a breach of contract arising from any:
- unilateral variation of an express term in their contract of employment
- breach of an implied term, such as the implied duty of trust and confidence.

New employees are protected from less favourable treatment on the grounds of being a:
- part-time employee
- fixed-term employee.

Breach of contract can result in the following penalties:
- £25,000 maximum for breach of contract claims heard at tribunal, e.g. those arising or outstanding on termination of employment
- unlimited compensation for a claim brought in a county court or the High Court, e.g. those involving a covenant in restraint of trade or intellectual property rights.

Less favourable treatment of part-time and fixed-term employees can result in:
- an award of unlimited compensation.

2.2. AUTOMATICALLY UNFAIR DISMISSAL

2.2.1. Automatic right to be protected from unfair dismissal

This right applies to reasons connected with:

- discrimination on the grounds of sex, sexual orientation, race, religion or belief, disability, married or civil partnership status, gender reassignment and age
- asserting a relevant statutory right
- trade union membership, participation or refusal to join a trade union
- trade union recognition
- certain health and safety matters
- pregnancy, childbirth, maternity leave, parental leave, dependant's leave
- the enforcement of the **Working Time Regulations 1998**
- the performance of duties as a pension scheme trustee
- the performance of duties as an employee representative
- making a protected disclosure (under whistle blowing legislation)
- asserting rights in connection with the National Minimum Wage
- carrying out jury service
- exercising the right to be accompanied to a disciplinary/grievance hearing
- taking part in official industrial action
- asserting certain rights as a part-time worker
- asserting certain rights as a fixed-term employee
- enforcing rights to Working Tax Credits
- an application for flexible working
- the statutory information and consultation procedure
- selection for redundancy on any of the above grounds.

Note. There are two other areas where employees are protected against automatically unfair dismissal: performing functions in relation to the **Transnational Information and Consultation of Employees Regulations 1999** and for reasons relating to the **European Public Limited - Liability Company Regulations 2004**. But these are unlikely to be relevant to small businesses.

What are the risks?

Unlimited compensation where the dismissal is connected with discrimination on the grounds of sex, sexual orientation, race, religion or belief, disability, married or civil partnership status, gender reassignment and age, health and safety or if it falls within whistle blowing provisions.

For all the rest, the maximum a tribunal can award is £76,700 (comprised of a basic award of up to £11,400 and a compensatory award of £65,300).

A tribunal order to reinstate or re-engage the employee.

An additional award can also be made where a tribunal originally ordered re-instatement or re-engagement and it's not complied with. Where this applies, it will be between £9,880 and £19,760.

If an employee is dismissed for trying to enforce any of the rights listed above, they can mount an automatically unfair dismissal claim against you. This would be brought at an employment tribunal and any financial award made would be comprised of two elements. The first is a "basic award", designed to compensate the employee for loss of job security. It's calculated in the same way as a statutory redundancy payment, i.e. on the basis of the employee's age and years of service multiplied by a maximum weekly amount, which is currently capped at £380. So the maximum amount that can be awarded under a basic award is £11,400.

In addition to this, there's a compensatory award that's designed to reflect both immediate and future loss of earnings. The current maximum award is £65,300; due to changes in the Retail Price Index it has decreased from £66,200.

Note. There are two exceptions to this: **(1)** where a dismissal is on health and safety grounds; or **(2)** if it's connected with the whistle blowing provisions of the **Public Interest Disclosure Act 1998**. In these cases (as with discrimination), a tribunal can award an uncapped amount of compensation.

A tribunal can also order reinstatement or re-engagement. Reinstatement is where the employee returns to their old job and is treated as if the dismissal had never occurred. They will be compensated for any loss of pay and benefits from the date of their dismissal and until the reinstatement takes place.

If re-engagement is ordered, you would be expected to re-employ the dismissed employee but not necessarily in their original role, or even under the same terms and conditions.

However, the good news is that, in practice, the tribunal rarely orders reinstatement. This is because, in most cases, the working relationship will have broken down irretrievably and it's not viable for the dismissed employee to return to their old workplace in any capacity. However, if on the rare occasions such an order is made and the employer refuses to comply without good reason, the tribunal can make an additional award of compensation. If so, it will vary from 26 to 52 weeks' pay.

Example

26 weeks @ £380 per week = £9,880
52 weeks @ £380 per week = £19,760

How does it work?

The usual requirement of one year's continuous service to qualify for unfair dismissal rights doesn't apply. Instead, the statutory rights outlined above are considered to be sufficiently important that an employee gains immediate protection from dismissal for trying to exercise one or more of them.

An employee can't waive their rights from day one under any circumstances and protection from automatically unfair dismissal is afforded in each of the following areas:

- **Discrimination on grounds of sex, sexual orientation, race, religion or belief, disability married or civil partnership status, gender reassignment and age.** If you dismiss an employee on one of these grounds, e.g. because they are a woman or due to a physical impairment, it's automatically unfair.

- **Asserting a relevant statutory right.** You can't dismiss an employee because they insist that you abide by a particular legal requirement in relation to their employment, e.g. granting 5.6 weeks holiday for those who work a five-day week (pro rata for part-timers) and the right to refuse to opt out of the 48-hour week. Protection is afforded by s.104 of the **Employment Relations Act 1996** (ERA).

- **Trade union (TU) membership, participation or refusal to join.** New employees are protected by s.152 of the **Trade Union and Labour Relations (Consolidation) Act 1992** (TULRCA) should they refuse to join a union, or if they choose to join one.

- **TU recognition.** Any dismissal of a new employee for involvement in certain functions relating to obtaining TU recognition is protected by Schedule A1 para 161 of TULRCA.

- **Performing certain health and safety duties.** Protection is afforded by s.100 of the ERA and includes where an employee is dismissed for proposing to carry out health and safety-related activities in connection with their job role, or raising concerns about health and safety matters.

- **Family-friendly rights.** A dismissal will be automatically unfair if it's for a reason connected with pregnancy, taking maternity leave and pay, paternity leave and pay, adoption leave and pay, childbirth and parental leave (under s.99 of ERA).

- **Enforcement of Working Time Regulations.** Employees are protected from dismissal for refusing to sign an opt-out agreement under the **Working Time Regulations 1998** or to forego a right to other provisions, such as breaks (s.101 of the ERA).

- **Performance of duties as a pension scheme trustee.** Employees acting as pension scheme trustees are protected from dismissal for performing or proposing to perform a function in relation to that appointment (s.102 of the ERA).

- **Performance of duties as an employee representative.** Any employee who is performing certain functions as an employee representative, e.g. during redundancy consultation, is protected under the **Transfer of Undertakings (Protection of Employment) Regulations 2006** (TUPE) or the collective redundancies legislation (s.103 of the ERA).

- **Making a protected disclosure.** Employees are protected under whistle blowing legislation - the **Public Interest Disclosure Act 1998** - and s.103A of the ERA.

- **Rights connected with the National Minimum Wage.** A dismissal will be automatically unfair under s.104A of the **National Minimum Wage Act 1998** if you dismiss an employee for asserting their right to receive the appropriate hourly rate for their age.

- **Carrying out jury service.** It's automatically unfair to dismiss an employee for taking time off work for jury service. However, a dismissal won't be unfair if your business would be badly affected by the employee's absence but they refuse or fail to apply to the court to be excused or to have their attendance deferred to a later date.

- **Exercising the right to be accompanied to a disciplinary/grievance hearing.** You can't dismiss an employee for exercising their right to be accompanied at either a disciplinary or grievance hearing under s.12 of the **Employment Relations Act 1999**.

- **Taking part in official industrial action.** Providing the industrial action is official, any dismissal of an employee for lawful participation is automatically unfair. This includes action lasting twelve weeks or less, or longer if you haven't taken reasonable steps to resolve the dispute.

- **Asserting certain rights as a part-time worker.** Regulation 7 of the **Part-time Workers (Prevention of Less Favourable Treatment) Regulations 2000** provides that it's automatically unfair to dismiss someone for asserting their right under this legislation.

- **Asserting certain rights as a fixed-term employee.** The same applies for dismissing an employee for exercising rights under the **Fixed-term Employees (Prevention of Less Favourable Treatment Regulations) 2002**.

- **Enforcing rights to Working Tax Credits.** You can't dismiss an employee if the principal reason relates to a claim made for Working Tax Credit (s.104B of the ERA).

- **An application for flexible working.** If an employee makes, or proposes to make, an application to work flexibly from day one, and they are dismissed on this ground, it will automatically be unfair (s.104C of the ERA). However, do note that an employee must have 26 weeks of continuous employment before they are entitled to be considered for a flexible working arrangement - but many ask before that!

- **The statutory information and consultation procedure.** Dismissal of an employee seeking to enforce rights under the Information and Consultation of **Employees Regulations 2004** (ICER) is automatically unfair. Since April 6 2008 these Regulations apply to undertakings with 50 or more employees.

- **Selection for redundancy on any of the above grounds.** If you attempt to disguise a dismissal as redundancy and it's for any of the reasons outlined above, it will be automatically unfair.

Should you dismiss an employee for exercising one of these protected rights, they have several options available to seek redress. The most common is to apply to a tribunal with the complaint. Alternatively, they could seek arbitration via ACAS, or agree to alternative dispute resolution in the form of mediation.

How to avoid it?

Apart from being aware of the list of activities that gives rise to legal protection from day one, you also need avoid certain types of behaviour. For example:

- **Discrimination on grounds of sex, sexual orientation, race, religion or belief, disability married or civil partnership status, gender reassignment and age.** Whilst this is becoming less common due to increasing awareness amongst employers of discrimination law, never dismiss an employee for one of these reasons. Instead, and assuming that the situation merits it, rely on one of the other potentially fair reasons for dismissal, such as conduct, capability or "some other substantial reason". A robust equal opportunities and dignity at work policy can outline how all staff will be treated. Simply having one in place will show that you take this issue seriously.

Download Zone

For an **Equal Opportunities and Dignity at Work Policy**, visit **http://books. indicator.co.uk**. You'll find the access code on page 2 of this book.

Employer tip

With age discrimination, the default retirement age is still 65, therefore you won't run the risk of the dismissal being deemed to be automatically unfair. The process and the law can be set out in a retirement policy.

Download Zone

For a **Retirement Policy**, visit **http://books.indicator.co.uk**. You'll find the access code on page 2 of this book.

- **Asserting a relevant statutory right.** You can avoid coming unstuck with this by not dismissing an employee simply because they insist that you abide by a particular legal requirement in relation to their employment. There are far too many statutory rights to list here, but some of the most common to watch out for are: **(1)** rights to minimum notice periods, e.g. one week's notice if the period of continuous employment is between one month and two years; **(2)** the right of a full-time employee to 28 days' annual leave; **(3)** the right to receive itemised payslips; **(4)** the right not to have an unlawful deduction made from wages; and **(5)** the right to refuse to opt out of the 48-hour week. The rights to paid statutory holiday can be set out in a holidays policy.

Download Zone

For a **Holidays Policy**, visit **http://books.indicator.co.uk**. You'll find the access code on page 2 of this book.

- **Trade union (TU) membership, participation or refusal to join.** Problems are easy to prevent if you remember that you can't dismiss an employee for belonging to (or refusing to join) a trade union.
- **TU recognition.** Similarly, avoid potential claims by not trying to dismiss an employee for their legitimate involvement in obtaining TU recognition in your workplace.

EMPLOYER TIP

Tribunals take illegal dismissals of TU members very seriously, so if you need to dismiss for any reason, do ensure that you can do so under one of the potentially fair reasons, such as conduct or capability. Also make sure that you have solid evidence to back up any decision.

- **Performing certain health and safety duties.** Prevent problems by remembering that different categories of employee are protected. For example, TU safety representatives and employees appointed under the **Health and Safety (Consultation with Employees) Regulations 1996** can't be lawfully dismissed for performing or proposing to perform a duty in relation to their role. Where no such representative exists, employees making their employer aware of a harmful or potentially harmful situation are also protected.

EMPLOYER TIP

An employee is also legally protected (by s.100 of the ERA) for leaving their workplace if they reasonably believe that there's "serious and imminent danger" that they can't be reasonably expected to avert, e.g. a toxic chemical leak.

- **Family-friendly rights.** As with previous examples, the easiest way to prevent an automatically unfair dismissal claim is to not dismiss an employee on one of the protected grounds, e.g. a reason connected with pregnancy, taking maternity leave and pay, paternity leave and pay, adoption leave and pay, childbirth and parental leave. But you can also outline their rights in clear policies.

Download Zone

For a **Maternity Policy**, visit **http://books.indicator.co.uk**. You'll find the access code on page 2 of this book.

Download Zone

For a **Paternity Leave Policy**, visit **http://books.indicator.co.uk**. You'll find the access code on page 2 of this book.

Download Zone

For a **Parental Leave Policy**, visit **http://books.indicator.co.uk**. You'll find the access code on page 2 of this book.

Download Zone

For a **Flexible Working Policy**, visit **http://books.indicator.co.uk**. You'll find the access code on page 2 of this book.

EMPLOYER TIP

For both adoption and paternity leave, the employee must have 26 weeks of continuous service before taking the leave. However, the right also protects an employee with less service should they announce that they intend to exercise their right once they have gained sufficient length of service.

- **Enforcement of Working Time Regulations.** This is another area that tribunals tend to penalise employers for ignoring. So stay out of trouble by not dismissing an employee for refusing to work in excess of a 48-hour week, for taking statutory breaks or for insisting on the statutory right to a health assessment if they are a night worker.

- **Performance of duties as a pension scheme trustee.** Don't dismiss an employee who is acting or who proposes to act in accordance with their role as a pension scheme trustee. These duties include, but aren't confined to, ensuring that employer contributions are paid when they are due, that the right benefits are paid out on time and that annual reports are prepared.

- **Performance of duties as an employee representative.** Employee representatives will be automatically protected against unfair dismissal if the reason relates to how they carry out their role in terms of consultation, e.g. over a transfer of undertakings or in redundancy consultations. Protection will also be afforded where they make their own representations on behalf of staff, e.g. making proposals that would avoid/reduce the number of redundancies.

- **Making a protected disclosure.** A protected disclosure is where an employee discloses information relating to a crime, miscarriage of justice, breach of legal obligation, danger to health, safety or the environment, and the concealment of evidence relating to any of these. However, in order to be protected from automatically unfair dismissal, the employee must be acting in good faith. They must also have reasonable grounds for believing that the information that they disclose indicates the existence of wrongdoing.

- **Rights connected with the National Minimum Wage.** Avoid problems by being aware of the correct minimum wage for an employee's age. From October 1 2009, the three hourly rates are: £5.80 for those aged 22 and over, £4.83 for those aged between 18-21, and £3.57 for those aged 16 or 17.

- **Carrying out jury service.** Don't forget that you only have a limited right to dismiss an employee for carrying out jury service. This is where your business would be badly affected by the employee's absence, but they refuse or fail to apply to the court to be excused or to have their attendance deferred to a later date. You can outline the rights in a leaves of absence policy.

Download Zone

For a **Leaves of Absence Policy**, visit **http://books.indicator.co.uk**. You'll find the access code on page 2 of this book.

EMPLOYER TIP

Avoid a finding of automatically unfair dismissal by ensuring that you can show you have provided evidence to the employee as to why their attendance would cause your business a problem.

- **Exercising the right to be accompanied to a disciplinary/grievance hearing.** This right to be accompanied is absolute and you can't put pressure on an employee to waive this right, never mind dismiss for it.

- **Taking part in official industrial action.** Before contemplating dismissal, ensure that the industrial action is official. This means checking that balloting requirements have been complied with and sufficient notice periods of any action have been given to you. If it's legal, then you can't dismiss on these grounds.

Note. If you have recently recognised a TU for the first time and are unfamiliar with the process, download the Code of Practice on "Industrial action ballots and notice to employers" for free from **http://www.berr.gov.uk/files/file18013.pdf**.

- **Asserting certain rights as a part-time worker.** Part-time workers are entitled to have equal access to any benefits that are paid to full-time staff who are comparators. So you can't dismiss an employee for asserting their right. All you can do is see if you can justify non-payment for a reason that's unconnected to working part-time, e.g. a difference in skills.

- **Asserting certain rights as a fixed-term employee.** The same principles apply to those working under fixed-term contracts.

- **Enforcing rights to Working Tax Credits.** Avoid problems by ensuring that you don't dismiss an employee who is, or may be, entitled to receive Working Tax Credits. Any employee that qualifies is free to enforce their right to this benefit.

- **An application for flexible working.** Do note that the one-year qualifying period no longer applies to this type of claim. Therefore, any attempt to dismiss an employee for making (or proposing) to make a flexible working application will be automatically unfair; however, the requirement to have 26 weeks of continuous service before the request can be granted still remains. So if problematic, focus on using one or more business grounds to refuse it.

Download Zone

For a **Flexible Working Policy**, visit **http://books.indicator.co.uk**. You'll find the access code on page 2 of this book.

- **The statutory information and consultation procedure.** If you have 50 or more employees, you don't have to consider this unless at least 10% of your workforce make a formal request.

  #### EMPLOYER TIP

  If you fail to comply with a request to set up consultation under the **Information and Consultation of Employees Regulations 2004**, you could face a fine of up to £75,000. This is in addition to any compensation that a tribunal could award for dismissal in connection with this statutory right.

- **Selection for redundancy on any of the above grounds.** Avoid allegations of automatically unfair dismissal by ensuring that any selection criteria for redundancy are transparent and that employees understand how the pool of employees was created. In fact, the more impartial the evidence, the less likely it will be that you will be challenged. You can outline the process in a redundancy policy.

Download Zone

For a **Redundancy Policy**, visit **http://books.indicator.co.uk**. You'll find the access code on page 2 of this book.

Trap. You can't negotiate with an employee to waive any of their statutory rights under any circumstances. Any agreement to do so will be void.

KEY POINTS

From day one, employees are automatically protected from unfair dismissal on the grounds of:

- discrimination due to sex, sexual orientation, race, religion or belief, disability married or civil partnership status, gender reassignment and age
- asserting a relevant statutory right
- trade union membership, participation or refusal to join a trade union
- trade union recognition
- certain health and safety matters
- pregnancy, childbirth, maternity leave, parental leave, dependant's leave
- enforcing the Working Time Regulations 1998
- performing duties as a pension scheme trustee
- performing duties as an employee representative (e.g. under ICER 2004)
- making a protected disclosure (under whistle blowing legislation)
- rights in connection with the National Minimum Wage
- carrying out jury service
- exercising the right to be accompanied to a disciplinary/grievance hearing
- taking part in official industrial action
- asserting certain rights as a part-time worker
- asserting certain rights as a fixed-term employee
- enforcing rights to Working Tax Credits
- an application for flexible working
- the statutory information and consultation procedure
- selection for redundancy on any of the above grounds.

Automatically unfair dismissal can result in the following penalties:

- unlimited compensation where the dismissal is connected with discrimination on the grounds of sex, sexual orientation, race, religion or belief, disability, married or civil partnership status, gender reassignment and age, health and safety or falls within whistle blowing provisions
- for the rest, a maximum award of £76,700 (comprised of a basic award of up to £11,400 and a compensatory award of £65,300). In some cases, there's a minimum award
- a tribunal order to reinstate or re-engage the employee
- an additional award may also be made where an order for re-instatement or re-engagement is made but not complied with. If this applies, this extra award will be between £9,880 and £19,760.

2.3. PAY-RELATED

2.3.1. Failure to provide an itemised payslip

What's the risk?

A tribunal declaration on what information your payslips must include.

How does it work?

By law, employees are entitled to receive an itemised pay statement that details both their gross and net pay and shows any deductions that have been made. This is a requirement of s.8 of the **Employment Relations Act 1996** (ERA) and it applies equally to part-time employees, irrespective of the number of hours worked.

How to avoid it?

You can easily avoid problems by providing an itemised pay statement either on or before the date payment is due. For example, if you pay on the 25th, then it must be received by the employee either on or before that date (not after). You need to ensure that the following details are included:

- gross pay
- any deductions that have been made, e.g. income tax and NI contributions
- net pay
- the amount of, and reason for, any variable deductions
- breakdown of net payments, where applicable, e.g. if wages are paid part-cheque and part-BACS into an employee's bank account.

2.3.2. Failure to pay the National Minimum Wage (NMW)

What's the risk?

An employee can reclaim all unpaid arrears at the applicable NMW rate.

A separate civil penalty levied by HMRC that represents 50% of the total underpayment. There's a minimum penalty of £100 and a maximum of £5,000.

Unlimited compensation for six criminal offences related to the NMW.

Any failure to pay the NMW carries two separate threats. The first is that an employee who believes that they aren't being paid the NMW can bring a tribunal claim against you in order to reclaim unpaid arrears. The second is rather more serious and relates to the potential involvement of HMRC in its role as enforcer of the NMW legislation. If it's made aware of a payment problem, e.g. via a tip-off or a complaint from the employee, it can levy a civil penalty in addition to demanding the payment of arrears.

This penalty will vary from £100 to £5,000. However, if you pay both the arrears and the penalty within 14 days of the date on which the notice of underpayment was served, you will only be required to pay 50% of the penalty. However, there are further criminal penalties which are reserved for the worst offenders. They will be used where there has been:

- a refusal or wilful neglect to pay the NMW

- a failure to keep sufficient NMW records

- false records kept

- false records or information produced

- the intentional obstruction of a compliance officer

- a refusal or neglect to give information to a compliance officer.

Note. These criminal offences will be heard in the Crown Court, not a magistrates' court, due to the possibility of an unlimited fine.

How does it work?

Since the **National Minimum Wage Act 1998** was introduced, there are three levels of minimum wage depending on the age of the employee. The current hourly rates are £5.80 for those aged 22 and over (the adult rate), £4.83 for those aged between 18 and 21, and £3.57 for those aged 16 or 17 (the development rate).

The rates are reviewed annually and any increases become effective from October 1. They apply to workers, including casual workers and temps, in the same way as they do for employees. However, the NMW does not currently apply to apprentices under the age of 19, or those who are aged over 19 and in the first twelve months of their apprenticeship. However, this will change from October 2010 when these categories of apprentice will receive a new minimum wage of £2.50 per hour.

Note. Another change from October 2010 is that the adult rate will be payable to those aged 21 and over (instead of aged 22 and above). NMW rates will also then increase to £5.93 for workers paid the adult rate, £4.92 for those aged 18 to 20 and £3.64 for those aged 16 and 17.

How to avoid it?

The easiest way of avoiding problems is to ensure that you are paying the correct rate appropriate to the age of each individual employee. You also need to keep records to confirm this. Whilst there's no legal definition of what is deemed to constitute a "sufficient" record, full payroll records should suffice. These can either be in a computerised or paper format.

EMPLOYER TIP

Whilst NMW records must be kept for at least three years by law, consider keeping them for six years, as workers have up to six years within which to bring a civil claim for failure to pay the NMW.

2.3.3. Failure to pay Statutory Sick Pay (SSP)

What's the risk?

Maximum penalty of £3,000 for a refusal or repeated refusal to pay SSP.

Maximum penalty of £3,000 for failing to keep records.

The purpose of SSP is to provide financial support to employees who are absent from work through sickness or injury. It's paid where there's either no occupational sick pay scheme in place, or where an employee isn't eligible to join it, e.g. during probation. Employees become eligible for SSP from the first day of their employment with you, providing that their average weekly earnings are a minimum of £97.00 per week gross. However, problems with its payment often arise due to confusion over entitlement and when it's triggered.

Note. More information on other penalties for breaches of SSP requirements can be found at **http://www.hmrc.gov.uk/employers/sp-penalty-offences.pdf**.

How does it work?

The current SSP rate payable for 2010/11 remains at £79.15 per week; the same as for 2009/10. The test for payment is simply that the employee has to be "incapable" of work. In terms of documentation, you are also required by HMRC to maintain detailed records of any SSP payments made.

An employee must be sick for at least four consecutive days (including weekends) before they can receive SSP. The first three days are known as the "waiting days"(WD), and whilst entitlement to SSP starts to accrue, no actual payment is made for this period. This is to enable more minor ailments to be eliminated. If an employee is still absent on the fourth day, then they are entitled to receive SSP. This fourth day is known as a "qualifying day" (QD).

SSP is payable for a maximum of 28 weeks. You can calculate the exact amount of SSP payable by using the free payment calculator at **http://www.hmrc.gov.uk/calcs/ssp.htm**.

An employee must be absent for three full days before the right to receive payment kicks in. So if they work in the morning before going home sick, that day won't count as the first WD.

Example

Bob's working week is Monday to Friday. He turns up to work Monday morning, but goes home at lunchtime and is off sick for the rest of the week.

Monday is not included in the calculation as Bob was not absent for a full day.

WDs = Tuesday - Thursday inclusive.

QDs = Friday (one day in total).

So Bob has one day's entitlement to SSP = £15.83 (based on £79.15 divided by five days).

In terms of evidence, employees should self-certify for any absence lasting one to seven days. An absence lasting longer than seven consecutive days should be accompanied by the new GP fit note.

Note. You can't withhold SSP for late receipt of medical evidence but you can do so for late notification of sickness. This is because the employee could have genuine problems in getting an appointment with a GP or if their illness unexpectedly continues into the eighth day.

Download Zone

For a **Self-Certification Sickness Absence Form**, visit **http://books.indicator.co.uk**. You'll find the access code on page 2 of this book.

How to avoid it?

If you doubt that an employee's claim for SSP is genuine, e.g. because another employee claims that the "sick" employee was moonlighting on a second job or was seen doing a strenuous workout at the gym, you need to investigate before withholding SSP. You should then meet with the employee to allow them to give their version of events; after all, it's possible that there's an innocent explanation.

But if you then decide to withhold all, or part, of the SSP for the period claimed, you must have solid evidence before doing so. This could be via a statement written by the employee who made the allegation that the absence wasn't genuine.

EMPLOYER TIP

If you only dispute part of the period that SSP is claimed for, write to the employee stating the days of absence and beside each, a note as to whether or not SSP will be paid for that day. If not, clearly set out your reasons why.

Should the employee still insist that they were genuinely sick, they should invoke your grievance procedure. They can also contact HMRC for a decision by an independent adjudicator. Where this happens (and you can't prevent it), both you and the employee will need to submit written evidence. If the adjudicator finds in favour of the employee, there's a right of appeal, but do consider if it's really going to be worth the extra time and trouble.

Download Zone

For a **Grievance Procedure**, visit **http://books.indicator.co.uk**. You'll find the access code on page 2 of this book.

EMPLOYER TIP

If you only pay SSP, consider amending your sickness policy to make it clear that you won't pay it for any days where you have good cause to doubt if some or all of the absence was genuine.

Example

"We will withhold the payment of Statutory Sick Pay (SSP) where we have good reason to believe that you were not incapable of work through illness on one or more of the days being claimed for. Where agreement can't be reached on this, you have the right to contact HM Revenue & Customs for an impartial decision by an independent adjudicator."

You can do much to avoid uncertainty and potential problems by using your staff handbook to clarify exactly how SSP works. You could also include your rules on notification of sickness absence. For example, even though for SSP purposes, you can't insist that employees personally notify you of any absences, or contact you more than once a week during the absence, you can introduce your own rules, e.g. daily phone calls by 9.30am on each day of absence.

In terms of record-keeping, you can do much to avoid falling foul of HMRC's reporting requirements by keeping details of the following:

- all dates of sickness absence lasting four or more days in a row for all employees
- a record of the payment dates and the amount paid during each "period of incapacity for work" (PIW)
- the date the pay period began
- a record of any unpaid SSP with the reasons.

EMPLOYER TIP

These records must be kept for at least three years after the end of the tax year they relate to.

Note. More information on employers' sickness absence records can be found at **http://www.hmrc.gov.uk/employers/employee_sick.htm**.

2.3.4. Unlawful deductions from wages

What's the risk?

Unlimited compensation.

Statistics for 2008/9 show that 33,839 claims for unlawful deductions from wages claims reached tribunal, so this remains a high-risk area. These claims are most likely to occur when you try to deduct a sum of money from an employee's salary or wages; often in an attempt to make up for a salary overpayment or to compensate for some other loss, e.g. to refund company sick pay that has been dishonestly obtained. But if you haven't retained the contractual provision to make such a deduction - irrespective of whether it's justified - it will be unlawful.

How does it work?

Legitimate deductions aside, s.13 of the ERA protects all employees from having wage/salary deductions made for bogus reasons, such as a penalty for raising a grievance, or for trying to make deductions in areas where it's illegal to do so, e.g. charging employees for personal protective equipment that's provided to them as a health and safety requirement. Under s.23 of the ERA, the amount awarded to an employee will be equal to that which was wrongly deducted, plus you will have to pay compensation to what, in practice, is often an undeserving employee.

How to avoid it?

You will need to identify all the individual circumstances where you wish to retain the right to deduct wages, i.e. create individual clauses. You also need to make it clear that you are only deducting a sum that represents your actual loss.

Whilst it may be tempting to make an extra deduction for the time and hassle that you've gone to, the law doesn't allow you to do this. So ensure that any deduction from wages clause clearly states it isn't an attempt to penalise the employee in any way.

Examples of the most likely scenarios where you should retain the right to make deductions are:

1. Leaving without giving sufficient notice. The most common scenario is where an employee leaves either without giving you any notice or without permission during the notice period. But providing you have a contractual provision, you're allowed to deduct a sum equal to a day's pay for each day not worked during the notice period. In practice, this provision will be better utilised for employees with notice periods of at least a month.

    Example

    "If you resign and leave without giving the required period of notice, or leave during your notice period without consent, the Company will be entitled to withhold one day's pay for each day not worked during your notice period. This is on the understanding that the Company will not deduct a sum in excess of the actual loss suffered by it as a result of your leaving without notice. Any sum so deducted will be in full and final settlement of the Company's claim for this breach of contract. The deduction will be made from any final salary payment which the Company may be due to make to you. Please note that the amount deducted is a genuine attempt by the Company to assess its loss as a result of your leaving without notice and is in no way intended to act as a penalty."

2. Dishonest claiming of sick pay. If you pay company sick pay, you may wish to restrict its payment in certain circumstances, particularly if you pay at three-quarters or full salary rate. You need to consider when this should apply and incorporate any exclusions into one clause. Examples include if an employee is caught fraudulently claiming sick pay when they are not sick or they have not turned up to work due to a hangover.

    Example

    "Staff should note that any payment of sick pay will be discretionary and is subject to several factors including where we have doubts as to whether the absence, or its seriousness, is genuine. A second is where it is a result of pursuing a dangerous sport. Where this applies, we retain the right to limit payment to.......... (insert period or amount). The Company also retains the right to take disciplinary action against any employee who it reasonably believes is fraudulently claiming Company sick pay. This does not affect your right to Statutory Sick Pay."

Don't forget that legal protection in respect of unlawful deductions from wages extends to workers and not just employees.

3. Damage to equipment. It's possible that employees will have the use of company equipment, e.g. for homeworking or if they travel on company business, and they could be entrusted with some high value pieces of equipment, such as laptops and mobile phones. If they (or a member of their family) damage or lose it, you don't want to be footing the bill for a replacement. So it makes sense to retain the right to make a deduction from salary should any equipment be: **(1)** stolen; **(2)** lost; **(3)** damaged through negligence or carelessness; or **(4)** deliberately damaged. Again, ensure that this provision is drafted so as to represent a genuine pre-estimate of the loss that you'll suffer. It can't be seen to be punitive even if it's invoked as a result of deliberate damage on the part of the employee.

Save time by listing the items that have been loaned to the employee and ask them to sign to confirm that they consent to a deduction equal to the value of the market value of the equipment (or cost of repair).

Example

"If you are allocated one or more items of office equipment for use at your home or away from the Company's premises, you will be asked to sign a form acknowledging receipt of it. By signing this form, you will also provide your written consent for the Company to deduct a sum equal to the market value of any item of office equipment (or the reasonable cost of repair, as appropriate) from your wages should it be lost, stolen or damaged whilst under your control due to your negligence or a deliberate or reckless act or omission or should you fail to return it to the Company either when demanded or in the event of the termination of your employment."

2.3.5. Right to receive equal pay

What's the risk?

Unlimited compensation.

The hourly pay gap between part-time women and full-time men is, on average, 39.4%. Whilst the discrepancies may be greater for lower paid and less skilled jobs, pay inequalities persist in higher paid and more specialist positions too, particularly in the financial sector. Also, whilst it's true that most of these claims are brought by public sector employees, particularly within local government, the private sector may not escape relatively unscathed for that much longer because the **Equality Act 2010** (EA) focuses on pay transparency.

How does it work?

Under the **Equal Pay Act 1970**, women are entitled to receive equal pay with men. This is not only in relation to equal pay for equal work but also for "work rated as equivalent" (where a job has been assessed as part of an employer's job evaluation scheme). Since 1983, women have also had the right to claim equal pay for work of "equal value" to that of a man in the same employment (or vice versa). This is triggered either where there's no one of the opposite sex engaged on "like work", or where there's no existing job evaluation scheme in place.

How to avoid it?

One way of greatly reducing the risk of an equal pay claim is to carry out an equal pay review. It aims to: **(1)** compare the pay of male and female employees doing the same or equal work; **(2)** investigate the causes of any gender pay gaps; and **(3)** close any that can't be adequately explained on grounds other than sex. Whilst there's no legal requirement on the private sector to carry them out, and the government hasn't proposed to change this - yet - there are advantages in carrying out a basic equal pay review. These are as follows:

- employees already have the right to issue you with an equal pay questionnaire. Although you don't have to complete it, failure to do so or being evasive with your answers, will allow a tribunal to take a negative view in the event an equal pay claim is brought against you

- when the EA comes into effect on October 1, any public sector clients that you have (or hope to have) are increasingly likely to ask if you have carried out an equal pay review

- the EA also prohibits pay secrecy clauses which could increase the likelihood of an equal pay claim; and

- there's a growing number of wage comparison websites available. The latest, Glassdoor.com **(http://www.glassdoor.com)**, allows current and ex-employees to post anonymous salary entries and company reviews which are then vetted for accuracy. Whilst the current focus is more on London salaries, this website is expanding and it's likely to become increasingly popular with employees wanting to benchmark their salaries by occupation and location.

If you want to confirm that you don't have any problems, carry out a pay review as follows:

Step 1. Scope of review. Begin by deciding the scope of your review, e.g. will it be one department or an entire site? Then consider if you will restrict it to comparisons between those doing like work or include those doing work of equal value. This refers to work that's different but which is of equal value in terms of the demands of the job, e.g. skills.

Step 2. Work of equal value. If you're going to include work of equal value, you need to identify jobs that require similar levels of effort, skill, knowledge and responsibility. Don't just rely on job titles; differences can emerge over time. Instead, look at the work actually being carried out by job holders.

Step 3. Job groupings. The most common types of distinct job grouping are, managers, supervisors, technical staff, clerical worker, sales staff and machine operators, but do be prepared to create others depending on the nature of your business. Don't just compare jobs within broad functions such as sales; look across your entire business. Create brief job descriptions as this allows you to identify if jobs involving different types of work have similar levels of knowledge and skills.

Example 1

A female office manager and a male production supervisor may actually be doing similar work, e.g. both provide technical advice and assistance, and both allocate and check the quality of work and monitor timekeeping.

Example 2

A female clerical worker and male warehouse worker may both need reasonable IT skills, good interpersonal skills for dealing with customer queries, basic numeracy and a good knowledge of your company procedures. Again, their work is similar.

Step 4. Pay information. Collect details on basic pay and total earnings, e.g. overtime payments, shift allowances and bonuses. Also identify what work-related benefits are received, e.g. pension and private medical care.

Step 5. Pay comparisons. For each job grouping that involves similar levels of skill and knowledge, assess if both the basic and total hourly earnings are the same. Also check that the same work-related benefits are offered and if so, if they're at a similar value.

Step 6. Reasons for pay gap. If you've identified any differences in hourly pay or benefits between employees doing jobs which involve similar skills and responsibilities, you will need to look into why this is, particularly if women are generally paid less than men. This could be for numerous reasons, e.g. because part-timers are paid less or only male workers receive shift allowances and performance-related pay.

Step 7. Justification. See if you can justify any pay differences that you find, e.g. you may need to pay a premium due to skills shortages, some work is physically far more demanding and some jobs have more responsibility etc.

Step 8. Action plan. If you've identified pay inequalities that you can't justify, you need to weigh up whether to ignore them and hope that you're not challenged, or put an action plan into place that will quietly balance out these inequalities over the longer term.

Irrespective of whether or not you carry out an equal pay review, you could still be challenged on equal pay. If so, you will have a defence to an equal pay claim if you can show that although male and female employees are being paid differently for doing similar or equal work, the reason is due to a "genuine material factor" (GMF). In order to be successful, this GMF must be: **(1)** significant and relevant; **(2)** a major cause of the difference in pay; and **(3)** it must apply to the job in question. However, any GMF defence used can't be directly or indirectly discriminatory on the grounds of sex. For example, you can't justify unequal pay between men and women by relying on historical pay differences which were inherently discriminatory. Such a scenario often arose where bonuses that were originally paid to men became absorbed into the pay structure of jobs still carried out mainly by men. Acceptable GMF defences to use are:

- market forces and skills shortages (this must be kept under review). Geographical differences, such as London Weighting
- anti-social hours - this could be shift premiums or extra payments because the work is very physically demanding or done under unpleasant conditions
- higher/professional qualifications, where there's a genuine need to have them
- "Red circling"- this often occurs where a formal job evaluation (popular in the public sector) has found that some employees have historically been overpaid. Often salary is protected for a fixed period until other salaries have caught up.

EMPLOYER TIP

If you have concerns about an equal pay challenge (or claim), focus your energies on showing the differences between the skills, demands and responsibilities etc. of the roles being compared.

2.3.6. A right to arrears of pay where an employer becomes insolvent

What's the risk?

No extra risk to you.

Hopefully, insolvency is something that you will not experience. Nevertheless, we are including this employee right.

How does it work?

If you become insolvent and an employee's employment is terminated, they may be entitled to recover some money from the National Insurance Fund. This would represent full or partial recompense for any money owing to them that you are unable to pay (s.182 ERA). In order to claim, an employee would have to apply in writing to the Secretary of State. No qualifying length of service is required and, at present, a claim could be made for the following:

- **Wages.** Up to eight weeks' wages paid at a maximum of £380 per week, giving a maximum of £3,040. This includes commission and overtime.

- **Holiday pay.** Any outstanding holiday pay for up to six weeks, up to the limit of £380 per week. This includes holidays taken but not paid, or any outstanding holiday leave that you have accrued. Income tax and NI at the basic rate will be deducted from this amount.

- **Notice pay.** An employee can also claim compensation if you fail to give the minimum statutory notice period. The maximum payable is £380 per week.

- **Unfair dismissal.** A basic award for any unfair dismissal may be paid.

Note. More information can be obtained from the Insolvency Service. It has produced a guide entitled "Redundancy & Insolvency: A guide for employees" which can be downloaded from: **http://www.insolvency.gov.uk/redundancyandinsolvency/ howdoiclaim.htm**.

How to avoid it?

The only way you can avoid this employee's rights being triggered is to successfully avoid insolvency!

With regards to pay, from day one, employees have the right to:

- receive itemised payslips
- the appropriate level of NMW for their age
- receive SSP if they fulfil eligibility requirements
- not have unlawful deductions made from their wages
- equal pay
- receive partial arrears of pay if you became insolvent.

Pay-related breaches can result in:

- a tribunal declaration regarding what information payslips should include
- an employee being able to reclaim all unpaid arrears at the current NMW rate
- a civil penalty for NMW underpayments of between £100 and £5,000
- unlimited compensation for six criminal offences related to the NMW
- a maximum penalty of £3,000 for a refusal or repeated refusal to pay SSP
- a maximum penalty of £3,000 for failing to keep records
- unlimited compensation for making an unlawful deduction from wages
- unlimited compensation for failure to provide equal pay.

2.4. FAMILY-FRIENDLY TIME OFF

Employees have two types of right from day one and these are broadly divided into two sections. The first relates to family-friendly rights and the second to time off for statutory duties.

2.4.1. Right to take up to 26 weeks' ordinary maternity leave, followed by up to 26 weeks' additional maternity leave

What's the risk?

Maximum £500 fine for allowing a woman to return within the period of compulsory maternity leave.

Unlimited compensation for sex discrimination.

The **Employment Relations Act** (ERA) provides for a period of compulsory leave which occurs immediately after giving birth, i.e. the woman is not permitted to work at all. Generally, it's two weeks but this is extended to four weeks for factory workers. In terms of sex discrimination, the risk tends to lie in pressurising a pregnant employee to curtail any period of maternity leave, or by subjecting her to a detriment for taking it, e.g. refusing a promotion or slashing any bonus payments that were earned before the maternity leave was taken. As only women fall pregnant, this will be deemed to be sex discrimination which automatically carries unlimited compensation.

How does it work?

All pregnant employees are entitled to a period of ordinary maternity leave (OML) for which there is no qualifying length of service. This lasts for 26 weeks and following that, the woman is also entitled to 26 weeks' additional maternity leave (AML). In terms of procedure, the pregnant employee must notify you of her intention to take maternity leave before the end of the 15th week before the expected week of childbirth. Her notification must include the date from which she intends to start her maternity leave, and this must not be earlier than the beginning of the 11th week before the baby is due. Within 28 days of receiving this notice, you must notify her of the end date of her maternity leave. During maternity leave, you are allowed to keep in touch with the employee and she is allowed to work for up to ten "keeping in touch" days during this time without her maternity leave coming to an end, or her statutory maternity pay being affected.

Note. If a woman is sick as a result of a pregnancy-related illness at any time during the final four weeks of her pregnancy, OML will be automatically triggered. In these circumstances, OML will start the day after the first day of sickness.

How to avoid it?

Apart from ensuring that the appropriate period of compulsory maternity leave is taken, you need to avoid putting any pressure on a pregnant employee for stating that she intends to exercise her right to take her full entitlement to maternity leave (or more time off than you would like). Equally, you must avoid subjecting her to any detriment for doing so.

EMPLOYER TIP

During the period of OML the employee is entitled to receive all her contractual benefits, except for salary. Therefore, both contractual and statutory holiday leave under the **Working Time Regulations 1998** will continue to accrue and she will also remain entitled to any benefits that she has been given as part of her job, e.g. the use of a car, laptop and any payment of professional subscriptions.

Also, women on AML are now entitled to receive all non-salary benefits. So this means that, in practice, the only difference between OML and AML is that if an employee returns after OML, she's legally entitled to return to the same job. This must be on no less favourable terms and conditions than she had before.

Should she return after AML has ended, you don't have to offer her old job back if it isn't reasonably practicable to do so, but you must offer an appropriate alternative. This means a job that is suitable for the employee's skills and knowledge and which isn't a demotion. You can do much to avoid this by planning for both the maternity leave and the employee's return:

Step 1. Get organised. Before the employee goes on maternity leave, establish how you will maintain contact with her. Also ensure that an appraisal is held, if due, and that any bonus owed is paid.

Step 2. Keep in touch. Don't forget to keep her informed about updates as well as job opportunities. Forward details of all jobs, as employers have come unstuck in tribunal for not doing this, even though the employee lacked the skills and experience to be considered for a position.

Step 3. Before the return. If an employee has taken AML and can't return to her old job, do explain why this is, e.g. due to restructuring. Always have solid evidence to back this up.

Step 4. Welcome meeting. On the first day back meet with the employee and set out what her priorities will be for the coming weeks. Also ensure that support is available.

A maternity leave plan can help you obtain most of this information, although an employee is under no obligation to complete it.

Download Zone

For a **Maternity Leave Plan**, visit **http://books.indicator.co.uk**. You'll find the access code on page 2 of this book.

2.4.2.   Time off for ante-natal care

What's the risk?

Refusal of paid time off - unlimited compensation for sex discrimination.

Giving unpaid leave - unlawful deduction from wages claim to which there is no defence.

Pregnant employees are entitled to time off to attend ante-natal clinics/classes. So if you refuse to grant this, or try to insist that time off is unpaid, the employee can mount a claim for sex discrimination (on the basis that only women can be pregnant and require these classes). The compensation is, of course, potentially unlimited as this amounts to sex discrimination. In addition, should you allow the leave but refuse to pay salary when it's taken, the employee can bring an unlawful deduction of wages claim.

How does it work?

A pregnant employee is entitled to paid time off for ante-natal appointments, providing that it has been made on the advice of a medical practitioner, registered midwife or a registered health visitor. Apart from medical appointments with consultants etc., it may also include relaxation and parentcraft classes. There is no prescribed amount of time that they are allowed to take but it must be sufficient for: **(1)** travelling to and from the appointment; **(2)** waiting time; and **(3)** attending the ante-natal clinic/class. Depending on the time of the appointment, you can reasonably expect the employee to attend work before and/or afterwards. If fathers wish to attend ante-natal appointments, you are well within your rights to ask them to make up the time later or to take annual leave. They have no statutory right to take it.

EMPLOYER TIP

Except for the first appointment, which you can't refuse, you are within your legal right to ask to see proof of subsequent appointments.

How to avoid it?

Problems can be avoided by allowing the employee paid time off to attend these appointments. However, you can ask them to try to make them at the beginning or end of the day in order to minimise disruption for you, particularly if you are a small business. If the pregnant employee is part-time, you are also within your rights to ask her to try to make ante-natal appointments in her own time.

EMPLOYER TIP

Alternatively, use a pro rata system. So if a part-time employee works three days a week, allow her to make 3/5ths of her appointments on work days.

Download Zone

For a **Maternity Policy**, visit **http://books.indicator.co.uk**. You'll find the access code on page 2 of this book.

2.4.3. Emergency time off to care for a dependant

What's the risk?

Compensation that is "just and equitable" for refusal to allow time off and subjecting an employee to a detriment for requesting dependant's leave.

Unfair dismissal - a maximum award of £76,700 (comprised of a basic award of up to £11,400 and a compensatory award of £65,300).

A tribunal order to reinstate or re-engage the employee.

An additional award may be made where an order for re-instatement or re-engagement is made but not complied with. If this applies, this extra award will be between £9,880 and £19,760.

If you unreasonably prevent an employee from taking dependant's leave, they can bring a claim within three months of your refusal. Should the complaint be successful, the tribunal will make a declaration to the effect that the employee was entitled to take leave in the particular circumstances and it may also award compensation. The amount will vary, but the tribunal will take into account your behaviour and motives in refusing the leave as well as any loss sustained by the employee. This could include injury to feelings. The issue of detriment is potentially more serious for employers. This could occur in many ways but common examples include refusing to promote an employee due to a request for dependant's leave, or denying them training opportunities as a result.

Note. Compensation will take into account the following: **(1)** nature of the breach and any loss sustained by the employee as a result; **(2)** expenses reasonably incurred; **(3)** loss of any benefit that the employee may have otherwise expected to receive; and **(4)** injury to feelings.

Under s.99 of the ERA and Regulation 20 of the **Maternity and Parental Leave etc. Regulations 1999**, employees are also protected against dismissal (including being selected for redundancy) if the reason or main reason was that they took or tried to take time off to care for dependants. If you dismiss under these circumstances, then it will be automatically unfair. However, if the employee has abused the statutory right to take dependant's leave, e.g. they went on holiday, and after following a disciplinary process you decide to dismiss, such a dismissal may be fair.

How does it work?

Under s.57(1) of the ERA, all employees have a right to take such "reasonable" time off from work as is necessary for dependants. For the purposes of the ERA, a dependant is a: **(1)** spouse; **(2)** parent; **(3)** child; or **(4)** a cohabitee (living in the same home as the employee). A cohabitee is defined widely under these Regulations and includes an elderly relative.

In addition, there's a catch-all category that includes anyone *"who reasonably relies on the employee to provide assistance or make arrangements"* (s.57A(3)-(5) of the ERA). Time off can be taken during working hours under the following circumstances:

- to provide assistance if a dependant falls ill, gives birth or is injured or assaulted
- in consequence of the death of a dependant
- to make arrangements for the provision of care for a dependant who is ill or injured, or
- to deal with an incident involving a child of the employee and which occurs unexpectedly at school etc.
- due to unexpected disruption or termination of arrangement for the care of a dependant, e.g. a childminder is sick or the school closes due to heavy snow.

Should an employee need to take time off, they must notify you as soon as is reasonably practicable. This does not have to be in writing but, in whatever form it takes, it should include an estimate of how long the absence will be. The phrase "reasonably practicable" is included as it's recognised that there may be exceptional circumstances when such notification isn't possible.

EMPLOYER TIP

If the employee doesn't provide notification as to the need for time off, be it at the outset or afterwards, the right to this time off is negated. This means that it must then be taken retrospectively as annual leave.

How to avoid it?

The vast majority of tribunal cases revolve around two issues. The first is the question as to what is deemed to be a "reasonable" period of leave and the second is whether or not the leave exists to allow employees to provide ongoing care for a dependant themselves. In terms of the first question, case law suggests that a reasonable period of leave will usually be one or two days. Any longer and you could require the employee to take the time off as annual leave. One or two days is normally sufficient to allow an employee to deal with the immediate crisis, e.g. to ensure that an elderly relative is not left alone and to also arrange alternative care arrangements. It's not for employees to provide the care themselves.

Also, until fairly recently, it was believed that requests made more than one or two days in advance wouldn't qualify as an emergency requiring dependant's leave. However, this changed after the case of Royal Bank of Scotland v Harrison 2009. In this case, Harrison (H) had been given two weeks' notice by her childminder that she couldn't work on a specific day. Although she tried to make alternative arrangements, she was unsuccessful. Her employer refused her the time off as it couldn't find someone to cover for her. She was also informed that any absence taken would be treated as unauthorised. H went ahead and took the leave which resulted in a formal disciplinary warning. Her appeal was unsuccessful so she took her employer to tribunal. The EAT decided that even where the requested time off was some way into the future, the disruption can still be "unexpected" and dependant's leave may be "necessary".

EMPLOYER TIP 1

Before refusing a request for dependant's leave, do find out the circumstances first. However, you can make it clear in your policy that employees are expected to explore all options for making alternative arrangements.

EMPLOYER TIP 2

Always keep good records of the amount of dependant's leave taken and the reasons for it, just in case you receive excessive requests from one employee.

Download Zone

For a **Time Off for Dependants Policy**, visit **http://books.indicator.co.uk**. You'll find the access code on page 2 of this book.

2.5 RIGHT TO TIME OFF

2.5.1. Entitlement to receive statutory paid holiday

What's the risk?

Failure to allow statutory holiday leave - enforcement by individuals in a tribunal.

Compensation at least equal to the amount of time off that has been refused.

Unlimited compensation for subjecting an employee to a detriment for asserting their right to this leave.

If you try to prevent an employee from taking the leave which they are entitled to under the amended **Working Time Regulations 1998** (WTR), e.g. by trying to get them to agree in writing that they will accept less annual leave, they are entitled to bring a tribunal claim to enforce their legal right to the full amount. Any claim must normally be brought within three months of the date that you allegedly made this refusal. If the complaint is upheld, the tribunal will make a declaration to that effect and will award the employee compensation to represent their lost leave entitlement. If the employee has sustained loss as a result, e.g. holiday costs, you will need to additionally compensate them. Furthermore, the tribunal can award compensation that it considers to be just and equitable in the circumstances.

Employees are also protected against detrimental treatment for asserting their right to receive their full statutory annual leave entitlement. Any claim must usually be brought within three months. If successful, a tribunal will make a declaration that the treatment amounted to a detriment, but more importantly it may award compensation. This is potentially unlimited and the amount awarded will take into account numerous factors, such as any expenses reasonably incurred by the worker, injury to feelings and loss of any benefit that they may have otherwise expected to receive, e.g. any bonus that might have been withheld.

How does it work?

At present, those entitled to 5.6 weeks' holiday a year include the following: **(1)** workers, e.g. anyone working under a contract of employment including employees; **(2)** agency workers; **(3)** non-employed trainees; and **(4)** agricultural workers. Since April 1 2009, all full-time employees and workers falling into one of these categories are entitled to a statutory minimum of 5.6 weeks' paid leave in each leave year. This works out at 28 days and applies irrespective of whether an employee works a five or six-day week. As this right to leave commences from day one of employment, entitlement to annual leave starts to accrue at the rate of one-twelfth of the annual entitlement on the first day of each month of that year in advance.

EMPLOYER TIP

The 28 days don't have to include bank and public holidays. When the leave is to be taken is a matter for you and your employees.

How to avoid it?

Whilst you can't prevent the leave from being taken at all, you can at least restrict *when* it's taken. This can easily be done by working on a first come, first served basis. You can also require employees to keep some leave free to cover annual shutdowns etc. However, you should first include a clause allowing you to do this:

Example

.... (insert number of days) of your annual holiday entitlement must be taken (e.g. during the off-peak summer months/at Christmas) when the Company operates a shutdown. The Company will give you notice of the exact dates you are required to take as annual leave as early as possible after the start of the holiday year and in any event at least one month in advance of the shutdown.

Another risk is being caught out by those who purport to be self-employed contractors, but later claim that they were in fact workers, thus entitling them to paid holiday leave. Since the statutory holiday entitlement was increased to 28 days per year, this has become an increasingly attractive option for try-it-on claims. In order to avoid this, you need to ensure that anyone you engage on a self-employed basis will work under a "contract for services". Apart from making sure that they look after their own income tax and NI payments, this contract for services must incorporate the following elements:

- it must state that it is a contract for services
- it must clearly describe the skills and experience that has led to the appointment
- that there's no mutuality of obligation, e.g. for you to offer work and for it to be accepted
- that there's a right to substitute labour
- if applicable, the individual must supply their own tools or similar equipment, e.g. laptop
- invoices must always be submitted before payment is made.

EMPLOYER TIP

Strengthen your position by making it a contractual requirement that you must agree to the individual being offered as substitute labour.

Another pitfall to avoid is giving statutory annual leave to those on long-term sick leave. This unfortunate state of affairs follows a European Court of Justice (ECJ) ruling in HM Revenue and Customs v Stringer. It was held that workers: **(1)** accrue statutory paid holiday whilst off sick; and **(2)** must be allowed to take this leave at some point in the future if they couldn't take it during their period of sick leave. As this ruling clashed with the provisions of the WTR, which require statutory leave to be taken in the year accrued, a decision had to be made on how this tricky issue should to be dealt with by employers. This was done by the House of Lords (now the Supreme Court), with the result that those on long-term sick are entitled to take holiday leave whilst sick and be paid.

2.5.2. To work, on average, no more than 48 hours per week with minimum rest periods

What's the risk?

Limits on weekly working hours, night work and record-keeping - criminal offence with a penalty of up to £20,000 in a magistrates' court or an unlimited fine in the Crown Court.

48-hour per week limit - enforcement by individuals at tribunal.

The Health and Safety Executive (HSE) is responsible for the enforcement of weekly working hour limits, night work (including various legal duties associated with night work), patterns of work and record-keeping. Failure to comply with any of these requirements can lead to a criminal prosecution and fine. The decision as to whether to prosecute in a magistrates' or Crown Court will depend on the seriousness of the breach. In terms of civil claims, individual workers will need to bring tribunal claims in order to enforce their legal entitlement to rest breaks and daily and weekly rest periods. This will be done in the same way as for enforcing the right to 28 days' annual leave (assuming that the employee is full-time).

How does it work?

From day one of employment, employees (and workers) become entitled to:

- work a maximum average of 48 hours unless the employee has agreed in writing to opt out. The average is usually calculated over a 17-week reference period
- a maximum limit of eight hours per day and 40 hours per week for young workers aged under 18
- a maximum average normal working hours limit of eight hours in each 24-hour period for "night workers"; again calculated over a 17-week reference period
- a minimum daily rest period of eleven consecutive hours a day for adult workers and twelve consecutive hours a day for young workers
- a minimum weekly rest period of at least 24 hours (or 48 hours in a two-week period) for adult workers, and 48 hours per week for young workers
- a maximum of eight hours' actual work in every 24 for night workers if their work involves special hazards or heavy physical or mental strain
- a prohibition on night work for most young workers
- a free health assessment for night workers and those about to start night work

- a rest break of 20 minutes for adult workers whose working day exceeds six hours, or 30 minutes where daily working time exceeds 4.5 hours for young workers

- 5.6 weeks' paid annual leave.

Working time includes any travel which is undertaken as part of an employee's job, such as sales staff travelling to see clients and potential clients. It also includes job-related training and working lunches.

EMPLOYER TIP

Working time doesn't include routine travel between home and work and rest breaks where no work is carried out.

How to avoid it?

In terms of working hours and rest breaks, compliance with the WTR will be achieved by ensuring that you comply with the requirements set out in the bullet points above. Yet whilst it very much depends on the nature of your business, one area where you may unwittingly come unstuck over excessive working hours is if you operate an "on-call" system, e.g. staff in a nursing home or engineers that may be called out in the event of an emergency. This is because of a landmark decision by the ECJ **(Landeshauptstadt Kiel v Jaeger 2003)** which held that if a job requires staff to be on call and at a place decided by you, e.g. at the workplace, then these hours count as work. This is the case even if the employee can sleep. As a result, the time spent on call counts towards total working hours. However, if you don't require the employee to be anywhere in particular, on-call time doesn't count unless and until they are called in or return to their normal working hours.

EMPLOYER TIP

Whilst you must keep up-to-date records of those who have opted out of the 48-hour week, you don't have to keep records of the hours worked.

You also need to take care over any night workers that you employ. A night worker is someone who normally works at least three hours between 11pm and 6am. As night work is known to be linked to certain medical complaints such as digestive disorders, the WTR require you to offer night workers a free health assessment. But this isn't the same as a full medical. Instead, a night worker's health assessment is in two parts: **(1)** a questionnaire; and **(2)** a medical examination. If an employee chooses to complete a questionnaire, a medical will only become necessary if sufficient concerns over their fitness to work are raised. These questionnaires are issued annually and all costs associated with them will be borne by you. In terms of record-keeping, you need to keep "adequate" records to show that the requirements relating to night work limits and health assessments are being complied with. These records must be kept for two years.

2.5.3. Time off for public duties

What's the risk?

Tribunal claim for declaration on suitable period for time off and possible compensation.

As an employer, you are under a statutory obligation to allow employees to take a reasonable amount of time off work to carry out "specified" public duties. If you don't, they can make a complaint to a tribunal. If it decides that time off was refused unfairly, it can make a declaration to this effect; this simply means written confirmation of your wrongdoing. But what it can't do is to give you binding directions as to the time off that you must allow the employee to take in future. An employee may also be awarded compensation, but the amount will be determined by what the tribunal considers *"just and equitable in all the circumstances"*, i.e. fair. As well as assessing any financial loss to the employee, the tribunal must also consider any stress, injury to feelings or loss of reputation caused by your actions.

How does it work?

The ERA sets out a specified list of public duties that an employee can request time off for. These duties relate to attendance at meetings or carrying out activities approved by the body in order to assist it in discharging its functions. This may include attending training courses. There are a number of public duties as follows:

- Justice of the Peace (lay magistrate)
- police authorities
- local authorities
- boards of prison visitors and prison visiting committees
- statutory tribunals, e.g. lay members of employment tribunals
- managing/governing bodies of educational establishments maintained by LEAs
- governing bodies and management boards of FE and HE colleges
- the General Teaching Councils for England and Wales and their Scottish equivalents
- NHS Trusts, Health Authorities and Health Boards
- Service Authorities for the National Criminal Intelligence Service or the National Crime Squad

- Environment Agency and the Scottish Environment Protection Agency
- water and sewerage authorities and Water Industry Consultative Committees.

The ERA doesn't specify the amount of time off that is allowed. This is in order to maintain flexibility, as different public duties will involve different time commitments. However, what will be deemed reasonable in the circumstances will involve consideration of your business and the impact that an employee's absence would have on its running. This was confirmed in the case of Borders Regional Council v Maule 1993 which involved a teacher who had taken 24 days off work in 1990 and 22 days in 1991 (at which point the school finally refused her any more time off). The EAT held that tribunals must take account of the number and frequency of any similar absences that an employee has had in connection with carrying out public duties. As a result, you will be protected from an employee who believes that they can take on various public duties as a means of avoiding work!

EMPLOYER TIP

This right to time off is unpaid.

How to avoid it?

You can avoid problems by being aware that an employee has a statutory right to time off in certain circumstances. Yet with regard to individual cases, this is not without limit. If an employee does request time off, work through the following steps:

Step 1. Is it covered? First, check that the time off requested is covered by s.50 of the ERA (see above). If it isn't, then you don't have to agree to it in work time.

Step 2. Future time commitment. Next, ask your employee for information on how much time off will be necessary in order to perform the duties of the office that they hold.

Step 3. Previous time off. Look at the amount of time that the employee has already been given as time off for public duties under s.50 of the ERA.

Step 4. Business needs. Finally, consider what the likely impact of the employee's proposed time off would be. This does not just refer to your staffing levels but also the employee's role in the running of your business.

You can set out how you will deal with a request in a leaves of absence policy.

Download Zone

For a **Leaves of Absence Policy**, visit **http://books.indicator.co.uk**. You'll find the access code on page 2 of this book.

2.5.4. Time off for duties as a trade union representative

What's the risk?

Tribunal claim for declaration of entitlement to time off and compensation.

If the employee has not been paid for the time off, compensation to reimburse them.

The risk to you centres on not allowing union representatives time off for trade union duties, which may be paid or unpaid depending on the activity.

How does it work?

If an employee is an official of an independent trade union that you formally recognise, they are legally entitled to take time off during working hours for union business. If they are involved with the following, this time off must be paid:

- attending meetings with management and members of the workforce

- accompanying workers to disciplinary and grievance meetings

- negotiating with you on terms and conditions of employment or disciplinary matters

- recruiting, organising and representing union members individually or collectively.

If union officials and members are involved in activities such as voting in union elections, meeting full-time officials to discuss workplace issues and attending meetings to discuss and vote on the outcome of negotiations, then the entitlement is to unpaid leave.

How to avoid it?

If you are a unionised workplace, or are in the process of recognising one or more trade unions, be aware that the right to time off for union duties does exist.

EMPLOYER TIP

More information can be found from the ACAS Code of Practice *"Time off for trade union activities and duties"*. It can be downloaded for free from **http://www.acas.org.uk/index. aspx?articleid=2391**.

2.5.5. Time off for duties as a trade union safety representative

What's the risk?

Compensation that is "just and equitable" for refusal to allow time off.

Compensation for failure to allow paid time off which is equivalent to the sum owed.

Under the **Safety Representatives and Safety Committees Regulations 1977**, any union-appointed health and safety representative is entitled to time off with pay: **(1)** during working hours as is necessary for them to carry out their functions; and **(2)** to allow them to be trained to perform their functions. This time off must be reasonable in the circumstances. Whilst these Regulations state that safety representatives should have at least two years' employment with you, it is acceptable for them to have two years' experience in a similar role. Equally, there's an exception in a new workplace where there's a high turnover or where the work is of short duration. It's for these reasons that there's no qualifying service before the right to time off in these circumstances is triggered.

Note. If you don't recognise trade unions but have elected representatives under the **Health and Safety (Consultation with Employees) Regulations 1996**, do be aware that they are also legally entitled to paid time off to carry out their duties and to undergo training to enable them to do so (Regulation 7). However, in comparison with union safety representatives, their functions are far more limited, e.g. they have no statutory right to be pro-active and make safety inspections; they can only make representations on matters that they become aware of.

How does it work?

Union-appointed safety representatives have certain statutory rights and functions that you can't limit in any way. The main ones are: **(1)** to investigate hazards and dangerous occurrences; **(2)** represent employees in discussions with you over health, safety and welfare issues and in discussions with enforcement authorities such as the HSE; **(3)** to attend safety committee meetings; **(4)** to investigate complaints; and **(5)** to carry out workplace inspections and to inspect relevant documents. Union safety representatives are generally entitled to as much time off as is necessary in order to perform their role.

EMPLOYER TIP

Do be aware that union safety representatives have duties only as employees. You can't hold them legally responsible if they fail to carry out their duties.

How to avoid it?

Again, just be aware that safety representatives (and employee representatives) have this right to time off. Therefore, you can avoid a claim by giving them paid leave to carry out their role.

EMPLOYER TIP

More information can be found by downloading *"Consulting employees on health and safety - a brief guide to the law"* for free from the HSE's website at: **http://www.hse.gov.uk/pubns/indg232.pdf**.

2.5.6. Time off to act as an occupational pension trustee

What's the risk?

Tribunal declaration that the time off should have been given.

"Just and equitable" compensation for failure to pay a trustee for the time off.

Any employee who has responsibilities as a pension fund trustee has the legal right to complain to a tribunal should you unreasonably refuse them time off to carry out their duties. They may also bring a tribunal claim if you allow them time off but refuse to pay them accordingly. The employee must bring a tribunal claim within three months of the date when the failure to give time off or to pay occurred.

If the complaint is upheld, the tribunal will make a declaration to that effect. However, if you haven't paid the employee, the tribunal can make an award based on what it considers as "just and equitable". The amount will be based on any loss to the employee, e.g. salary, but it may also include stress, injury to feelings or any loss of reputation due to your refusal. Where the tribunal claim has arisen out of your failure to pay, the tribunal is required to order you to pay the amount due.

How does it work?

If the employee is a trustee of an occupational pension scheme, or a director of a trustee company as defined by s.1 of the **Pension Schemes Act 1993**, they are entitled to take reasonable time off in order to carry out those duties. Equally, they are entitled to have time off in order to undertake training in how to undertake these duties.

How to avoid it?

A claim can be avoided by appreciating that any employee who is an occupational pension trustee has a legal entitlement to take time off and to be paid for doing this work. So, where possible, make a diary note of key meetings that an employee must attend and plan around it. Nevertheless, what is considered reasonable in terms of time off will partly depend on the needs of your business and the impact that the employee's absence will have on it.

EMPLOYER TIP

If you do have to refuse time off, explain why this is to the employee, e.g. some form of emergency or a very important client meeting that can't be rescheduled.

KEY POINTS

Employees have a statutory right to time off for:

- public duties (unpaid)
- occupational pension trustee work (paid)
- a role as a trade union representative (paid/unpaid depending on the duties)
- a role as a trade union safety representative (paid)
- looking after dependants (unpaid)
- statutory annual holiday leave (paid)
- rest and rest breaks (unpaid)
- maternity leave totalling 52 weeks (paid/unpaid depending on length of service)
- ante-natal appointments (paid).

If you refuse this time off, there are numerous penalties including:

- a tribunal claim for declaration on a suitable period of time off for public duties/compensation
- a tribunal claim for declaration on a suitable period of time off for pension trustee work
- "just and equitable" compensation for failure to pay a pension trustee for the time off
- a tribunal claim for declaration of entitlement to time off for union duties/compensation
- "just and equitable" compensation for refusal to allow time off for safety representatives
- "just and equitable" compensation for refusal to allow time off for dependant's leave
- a tribunal claim to enforce right to statutory holiday leave
- compensation at least equal to the amount of time off that was refused
- up to £20,000 fine in a magistrates' court for breaking limits on week hours/night work
- unlimited fine in a crown court for breaking limits on week hours/night work
- a tribunal claim to enforce right to work a maximum 48-hour week
- up to £500 fine for allowing a woman to return within compulsory maternity leave
- unlimited compensation for sex discrimination
- unlimited compensation for refusal of time off for ante-natal appointments
- unlawful deduction from wages claim for giving unpaid leave for ante-natal appointments.

2.6. WRONGFUL DISMISSAL

2.6.1. Protection from wrongful dismissal

What's the risk?

Unlimited compensation for breach of contract leading to the wrongful dismissal.

If the claim is for less than £25,000 it can be brought at a tribunal; if so, the employee has three months from the alleged breach within which to bring it. Claims over this amount can be brought in either a county court or the High Court, where legal costs may be recoverable by the successful party. The time limit for such claims is six years. In terms of compensation, the basic rule is that the employee needs to be placed in the same position that they would have been if the contract had been performed, e.g. if you had given the right notice. Should you dismiss the employee without first having gone through a disciplinary process, the compensation award is likely to be higher. This is because the damages will probably include the income earned during the time the disciplinary process would have taken to run (including the appeal). Plus, it could attract a compensation uplift of up to 25%.

Note. If the damages awarded exceed £30,000, the excess over that amount is taxable. So you could be required to pay an amount that is grossed up to ensure that the award received by the employee covers any tax liability to HMRC.

How does it work?

Wrongful dismissal refers to a contractual claim brought by an employee where there has been a contractual breach which resulted in dismissal. It most commonly occurs where you fail to give the correct length of contractual or statutory notice. It also might arise if you think that you can cut costs by dismissing an employee without providing adequate compensation in lieu of notice. In practice this is almost certainly guaranteed to backfire, as your ex-employee will not only claim for outstanding salary/wages but also for any other contractual benefits owing, such as accrued holiday pay, pension contributions and the benefits of any private health insurance. In addition, you will face the extra cost and time involved in dealing with a tribunal claim on top of what you would have paid had you complied with the notice requirements.

No minimum period of employment is required. This means that employees are protected in their first year of employment (though the right to a minimum notice period isn't triggered until the employee has a month's continuous employment - see Chapter 3).

How do you avoid it?

One of the easiest ways to avoid a wrongful dismissal claim is to look very carefully at the amount of notice that you require. For example, whilst notice periods of three or six months might be suitable for senior or highly specialist staff that could be difficult to replace, they're usually not necessary for other employees. In these cases, notice periods of one month should be sufficient. If you issue fixed-term contracts, do pay special attention to the notice periods that you give, as failure to include one means that you will be liable to pay the full length of the contract, e.g. you would have to pay four months' salary to a fixed-term worker on a six-month contract even if you dismiss them after only two.

EMPLOYER TIP

For staff on probation, keep notice periods short, e.g. one week.

The second risk area is benefits-in-kind. You should make the continuation of these benefits subject to the employee not having been given notice. For example, if you dismiss an employee with a company car who is entitled to three months' notice, but only give them one, they will be entitled to compensation for the two months that they don't have use of the car (though they're under a duty to keep those losses to a minimum). Instead, ensure that the right to these benefits terminates along with the ending of employment.

EMPLOYER TIP

Try to make as many benefits discretionary (non-contractual) as you can. This allows you to change or withdraw them without consultation.

2.7. GRIEVANCES

2.7.1. Right to raise a grievance and to be accompanied to a grievance hearing

What's the risk?

25% uplift to tribunal award for failing to hear a grievance or for failing to follow a reasonable procedure.

Up to £760 compensation for failing to allow an employee to be accompanied.

Since the old statutory disciplinary and grievance procedures were repealed in April 2009, a new non-statutory regime has taken its place. This is based on revised ACAS guidelines *"Code of Practice 1 - Disciplinary and Grievance Procedures"*. Under this Code, you can be penalised by an adjustment of up to 25% of any compensation award that you have to pay if you unreasonably fail to follow a provision laid down in it. Therefore, if you fail to offer a grievance procedure, or fail to follow a fair one, an uplift of 25% could be awarded. Common examples include not giving a right of appeal or insisting that the grievance is heard by the manager who is the source of the complaint. Another is to refuse an employee their statutory right to be accompanied. Should the employee bring a tribunal claim against you, they can be awarded compensation of up to £760 for your denial of the right to a companion. There's no minimum level of award and the £760 is based on two weeks' pay at the statutory amount of £380 per week.

How does it work?

The Code stipulates that the employee "should" inform you that they have a grievance. This means that informing you is no longer mandatory, so the first you may know of a problem is when a tribunal claim lands in your in-tray. On the other hand, the fact that an employee doesn't have to raise a grievance means you no longer need to waste time in trying to identify if a grumble is a formal grievance or not. Assuming that an employee makes you aware that there is a problem, and this should be encouraged, you should try to resolve it informally. However, if this isn't possible, then it should be dealt with at a formal meeting. If a grievance is related to a disciplinary matter, the two can be dealt with together. The right to be accompanied is statutory, so you can't create a grievance process that denies an employee this right.

How to avoid it?

If a grievance can't be dealt with informally, you can do much to reduce the risk of it turning into a tribunal claim by working through the following steps:

Step 1. Keeping you informed. Where an informal resolution isn't possible, employees should be encouraged to raise the matter formally rather than pursuing the tribunal route. This should be arranged with a manager who isn't the subject of the grievance and put in writing. The communication should set out the nature of the grievance, so encourage employees to give as much information as possible.

Step 2. Holding a meeting. Once you've been notified that an employee has a grievance, you need to arrange a formal meeting to discuss it. This should be done without "unreasonable" delay. No mention is made of what will be considered "reasonable", but within five days should usually suffice (allowing for annual leave or unplanned absences). As with disciplinaries, all parties are expected to make every effort to attend. At the meeting, the employee raising the grievance should be allowed to explain its nature and how they think it should be resolved. In the event that any investigation needs to be carried out, the meeting should be adjourned.

Step 3. The right to be accompanied. Employees have a statutory right to be accompanied by a companion at a grievance meeting providing that the meeting is to deal with a complaint about a duty owed by you as the employer (see below). Examples given in the new Code are where you aren't honouring the terms of the worker's contract or are in breach of legislation. The chosen companion may be a colleague, a trade union representative or an official employed by a trade union (providing that they have been certified by the union as being competent). In order to avail themselves of the right to be accompanied, the employee must make a "reasonable request". What will be considered reasonable will depend on the circumstances of each individual case. The companion may also address the hearing to put and sum up the worker's case, respond on their behalf to any views expressed at the meeting and to confer with them; they don't have the right to answer questions on the employee's behalf, address the hearing if the employee doesn't wish them to, or prevent you from explaining your case.

> **EMPLOYER TIP**
>
> As with disciplinary hearings, it would normally be deemed unreasonable for an employee to insist on being accompanied by someone whose presence would prejudice the hearing etc.

Step 4. Deciding on appropriate action. After the meeting, you must decide if you're going to take any action. Irrespective of what decision you reach, you need to write to the employee to let them know what will happen to resolve their grievance. This letter should inform them that they can appeal if they aren't happy with your proposed action.

Step 5. Appealing the grievance. If the employee feels that the grievance hasn't been resolved satisfactorily, they may appeal. This should be done in writing and include their grounds. Again, it should be done without "unreasonable" delay. Once you've received written grounds of their appeal, you're obliged to hear it without unreasonable delay. It should be at a time and place notified to the employee in advance. Wherever possible, the appeal should be dealt with impartially and ideally heard by a manager with no previous involvement in the case. Employees have a statutory right to be accompanied at any such appeal hearing. The outcome of the appeal should be communicated to the employee in writing and in a timely manner.

Step 6. Overlapping grievance and disciplinary cases. If the employee raises a grievance once the disciplinary process has started, the disciplinary may be suspended temporarily in order to deal with it. Where the two are related, the Code states that it may be appropriate to deal with the two together.

Download Zone

For a **Grievance Procedure**, visit **http://books.indicator.co.uk**. You'll find the access code on page 2 of this book.

2.8.   HEALTH AND SAFETY

2.8.1.   Failure to provide a safe system of work

What's the risk?

Up to twelve months' imprisonment for breaches of health and safety legislation.

And/or up to £20,000 fine in a magistrates' court.

Unlimited fine at Crown Court for the more serious health and safety offences.

Unlimited fine, imprisonment and Publicity Orders for offences of corporate manslaughter.

Since January 16 2009, fines for health and safety offences have increased thanks to the **Health and Safety Offences Act**. This Act amended s.33 of the **Health and Safety at Work etc. Act 1974** (HSWA) so that the maximum penalty which can be levied by the magistrates' court has risen from £5,000 to £20,000 for most health and safety offences. It also allows some offences that could only previously be tried in a magistrates' court to become triable at Crown Court. Also, imprisonment became an option for more health and safety breaches and it's now possible for magistrates' courts to pass a sentence of imprisonment. This is only for the most serious breaches, such as those under s.s.2-6 of the HSWA. Incidentally, the new penalties are not retrospective and will only apply to health and safety-related offences committed on or after January 16 2009.

Note. More information on the penalty regime can be found for free on the Office of Public Sector Information website: **http://www.opsi.gov.uk/acts/acts2008/ ukpga_20080020_en_2#sch1**.

As to be expected, the penalty regime is different under the **Corporate Manslaughter and Corporate Homicide Act 2007** (CMCHA). In 2010, the Sentencing Guidelines Council published its new guidance on how financial penalties should be calculated. Instead of a fine based on a percentage of turnover, Crown Court judges should work through the following stages: **(1)** consider the seriousness of the offence, e.g. the extent to which serious injury was foreseeable; **(2)** look at any aggravating or mitigating circumstances; **(3)** review the financial resources of a business by looking at the last three years' turnover, profit and assets; and **(4)** identify the impact that the fine would have on the "employment of the innocent", e.g. whether the proposed fine would put the company out of business. In terms of figures, it has been suggested that a fine under the CMCHA should be at least £500,000, running into millions for large companies. Finally, judges are encouraged to use their new powers to issue Publicity Orders. These are to be used in addition to financial penalties and should generally be used in all corporate manslaughter cases. As their name suggests, a company is required to actively publicise the fact that it has been convicted of a corporate manslaughter offence. This is likely to have a substantial effect on a company's financial position due to loss of reputation etc. In fact, it could prove as damaging as a large fine.

How does it work?

The main piece of legislation that refers to employers' legal duties in this area is the HSWA. This places a statutory duty on you to provide and maintain what's termed a safe system of work. This not only applies to industrial environments and construction sites, but also to lower risk environments such as offices. These safe systems of work need to be sufficient so they ensure, so far as is reasonably practicable, the health, safety and welfare of staff and others who can be affected by your activities. What is deemed reasonably practicable depends on your size as a business and your resources. Those covered by the HSWA include contractors working on your premises, visitors and members of the public. Whilst the HSWA is the main piece of legislation, there's a huge amount of health and safety legislation including provisions for display screen equipment, manual handling, provision and use of work equipment, personal protective equipment, workplace such as temperature and lighting, and the management of health and safety. Other regulations cover first aid and chemical use. Much of the legislation in this area is industry-specific, although it is down to you to ensure that you know which laws are relevant to your undertaking.

The risk of you facing a prosecution for corporate manslaughter is negligible. Nonetheless, the CMCHA makes it easier for a prosecution to be brought in the event that a death was caused by gross failings in how you run your business. Previously, it would have been necessary for the "controlling mind" of your business to be identified. This would be easy in a small business, but not in large businesses where responsibilities are often deliberately complex and blurred. In the event of a fatality all the prosecution now has to do is to prove beyond reasonable doubt that your business is directly responsible. A specific individual no longer needs to be identified.

EMPLOYER TIP

Just ensure that whichever individual is tasked with day-to-day health and safety responsibilities keeps your safety policy and risk assessments up-to-date.

How to avoid it?

Although the exact nature of your health and safely obligations will depend on your industry, there are a number of areas that you will need to cover, irrespective of whether you are a very small business or a large multinational.

The main ones are as follows:

- **Safe workplace.** You need to provide a workplace that is, as far as is reasonably practicable, healthy and safe. In practice, this means ensuring that any plant and equipment that you provide is safe to use and is well maintained. This includes regular checks of portable electrical appliances and adequate safety signage. It also requires you to maintain walkways, toilets, ventilation, heating and lighting.

- **Information.** You are required to provide employees, contractors and temporary staff with relevant information on health and safety. This can range from how to summon a first aider to the procedure for reporting a fire.

- **Training.** Health and safety training should be provided as part of induction training, even if it's only the basics such as fire evacuation procedures. It should also be provided if the nature of the job demands it. Do keep records of any training given.

- **Risk assessments.** Risk assessments need to be carried out and any significant findings recorded. Where possible, any risks identified should be eliminated, but where this isn't possible, they should be reduced "as far as is reasonably practicable". Due to the extra risks involved for pregnant, young or some disabled people, your risk assessments may need to cover them as appropriate. It's considered good practice to involve staff when carrying out risk assessments as they do the jobs/work in the areas being assessed.

- **Personal protective equipment.** Where risks can't be eliminated or controlled in any other way, you are required to provide personal protective equipment to staff, free of charge. This may range from safety footwear through to waterproof clothing and hard hats.

- **Health surveillance.** Some legislation, such as the Noise at Work Regulations, contains a requirement that health surveillance must be carried out for employees subject to certain noise levels. It might also need to be carried out if you have concerns about the ability of an employee to carry out their job safety.

If you employ more than five people, you also need to have the following in place:

- a policy statement that is signed by a senior director (preferably the managing director or chief executive) that outlines your organisation's commitment to health and safety. This should be reviewed annually, or more frequently, if there are major changes

- a health and safety policy that sets out how you manage health and safety. This will need to include the roles and responsibilities of directors, managers, supervisors and general duties on employees

- written health and safety documentation in place that demonstrates your approach to managing health and safety, e.g. a policy on how you manage contractors, organise first aid and how you report and record accidents/incidents

- means of measuring, auditing and reviewing your company's health and safety performance on a regular basis.

EMPLOYER TIP

You should review your safety policy annually or more frequently if there are major changes in your business, e.g. organisational restructuring.

Download Zone

For a **Health and Safety Policy**, visit **http://books.indicator.co.uk**. You'll find the access code on page 2 of this book.

From day one, employees are entitled to:

- protection against wrongful dismissal
- access a fair procedure for raising grievances
- bring a companion to a grievance meeting if it's connected with a complaint about a duty you owe to them
- a healthy and safe workplace.

Breaches can result in:

- unlimited compensation for breach of contract leading to the wrongful dismissal
- an 25% uplift to the award for failing to hear a grievance or following a reasonable procedure
- up to £760 compensation for failing to allow an employee to be accompanied
- up to a £20,000 fine in a magistrates' court for breaches of most health and safety legislation
- up to twelve months' imprisonment for serious breaches of health and safety legislation
- an unlimited fine in a Crown Court for the more serious health and safety offences
- an unlimited fine, imprisonment and Publicity Orders for offences of corporate manslaughter.

CHAPTER 3

First month of employment

After their first month in employment, employees accrue three further rights. The first two can be categorised as payments that are dependent on a particular event arising and the third is the right to be given a minimum period of notice should you need to terminate their employment for any reason.

3.1. PAYMENTS

3.1.1. Guarantee payments during lay-off or short time working

<u>What's the risk?</u>

Up to £21.20 per day (£106 for a maximum of five days in any three-month period).

The rate payable for guarantee payments has recently fallen and since February 1 2010 it's £21.20 a day for a maximum of five days in any three-month period (it was previously £21.50 for this period). The right to these payments (assuming basic qualifying conditions are met) is statutory. Therefore, if you fail to pay any amount owing to an employee that you are forced to lay off, they can bring a tribunal claim against you. This must be done within three months of your alleged failure to pay a guarantee payment.

<u>How does it work?</u>

If you become unable to provide an employee with work on any day that they would normally be required to work under their contract of employment, e.g. due to a decline in the type of work that the employee carries out, they may be entitled to a "guarantee payment" currently limited to a total of £106 (£21.20 x five days). During the period of lay off, there's no payment of actual wages.

But, there's an exception to this rule where an employee is part-time. Here, the entitlement to a guarantee payment can't exceed the number of days that they're required to work under their contract of employment. For example, if their contract requires them to work three days per week, the employee will only be entitled to three days' guarantee payment, i.e. £63.60.

Note. The term "lay-off" refers to a temporary situation where there's no work for an employee to carry out, and so a redundancy situation doesn't arise.

EMPLOYER TIP

If an employee's working week varies, the guarantee payment due is calculated by averaging out the number of days actually worked over the previous twelve weeks.

How do you avoid it?

In order to protect an employee in this situation, there are strict time limits that you must abide by. For example, once an employee has either been laid off for at least four consecutive weeks, or six weeks in a 13-week period, they may resign and serve you with written notice of their intention to claim a redundancy payment. However, they must have two years' continuous service to be able to do this.

In turn, you may serve a "counter-notice" within seven days of receiving this. However, this should only be done if you reasonably believe that you can provide a minimum of 13 weeks' continuous employment without having to resort to further lay-offs or short time working during that period. Also, due to the financial consequences for those affected, you must have retained the contractual right to lay off an employee, or put them on short time working. If you don't, it's likely this will be treated as a "repudiation of contract", i.e. an end to it, as you've tried to vary the employment contract unilaterally and without consent.

Note. This also means that if the employee has at least one year's qualifying service that they could claim constructive dismissal.

EMPLOYER TIP

If you have to lay off or put an employee on short time work, do keep good records of the days that they don't carry out any work.

Download Zone

For a **Lay-off and Short Time Working Clause**, visit **http://books.indicator.co.uk**. You'll find the access code on page 2 of this book.

3.1.2. Failure to pay a medical suspension payment to a qualifying employee

What's the risk?

Tribunal claim for the amount owed.

Providing an employee meets the eligibility criteria, they have a statutory right to be remunerated for up to 26 weeks if they are suspended from work on medical grounds. If you don't comply with this, they can bring a tribunal claim for failure to make a medical suspension payment. This should be brought within three months of the first day in which the employee alleges that you failed to make the payment.

Note. The tribunal has the discretion to extend this time limit if it wasn't reasonably practicable for the employee to bring a claim within the three-month time limit.

How does it work?

An employee is only entitled to be paid for up to 26 weeks if: **(1)** they are suspended on medical grounds; and **(2)** have at least one month's continuous service with you. However, this suspension must be for the purpose of complying with your obligations under health and safety legislation, e.g. exposure to hazardous substances such as chemicals under the **Control of Substances Hazardous to Health Regulations 2002 (as amended)** (COSHH). Alternatively, it may be to comply with a recommendation contained in a Code of Practice that has been approved under s.16 of the **Health and Safety at Work Act etc. 1974**.

Note. This right to be paid during a period of medical suspension relates to situations where your business is affected by the need to comply with specific health and safety legislation. It isn't driven by the state of the employee's health. For example, an employee working in a low risk office will not be entitled to paid medical suspension if they are suffering from respiratory problems, whereas they could be if they work in a factory that was covered by COSHH due to the type of chemicals used.

Similar rules apply if you need to suspend a pregnant woman or new mother from work on medical grounds. In these cases, the employee must be put on paid medical suspension if changing her working hours or providing alternative work isn't feasible, e.g. because there's no other suitable work available for her to do.

Employer tip 1

If you have engaged an employee on a fixed-term contract of three months or less, or on a specific task contract which isn't expected to last for more than three months, they aren't entitled to this type of payment.

Employer tip 2

Remuneration is a week's pay for every week of suspension (or pro rata for part-time employees). According to HMRC, these payments count as normal pay so must be taxed in the same way as if the employee was working. More information can be found at **http://www.hmrc.gov.uk/paye/exb/a-z/m/medical-suspension.htm**.

How to avoid it?

Assuming the employee has at least one month's continuous employment with you and fulfils the criteria, you need to pay them as you normally would. However, you are entitled to receive medical confirmation from their GP - in the form of the new fit note - or by obtaining specialist occupational health advice as to what alternative work could be carried out.

You don't have to make any payment at all if the employee unreasonably refuses a request by you to perform alternative duties.

3.2. NOTICE

3.2.1. Right to one week's minimum notice on the termination of employment

What's the risk?

Unlimited compensation for breach of contract.

If you fail to give an employee with at least four weeks' continuous service at least one week's notice, they could sue you for breach of contract. Whilst any sum recovered is likely to be fairly low for an employee who has only been with you for such a short period, the level of compensation is potentially unlimited. This is because it amounts to a breach of contract. Furthermore, the purpose of any award is to place the employee in the same position as they would have been had they been given the correct notice. So if they can't find alternative work, or have had to take a pay cut in a new role, you could be stung for the difference.

Note. Any employee who seeks to bring a claim with only one month's employment behind them will almost certainly refer it to tribunal (not the county or High Court) where the compensation limit is capped at £25,000. The amount claimed would generally be for any basic salary owed, but not paid, and the equivalent of any benefits that they would have enjoyed during the notice period.

How does it work?

Employees have a statutory right to receive at least one week's notice after one month of employment. Whilst you can offer more than that, e.g. via a more generous contractual provision, you can't offer less. It's for this reason that many employers limit the notice periods during probation to the statutory minimum and limit the benefits offered, e.g. no entitlement to bonus or commission payments and/or private health insurance until the employee has completed their probation period satisfactorily.

How do you avoid it?

As soon as a new employee has accrued one month's (four weeks') employment with you, they are entitled to one week's notice if you wish to terminate the contract. However, if you do wish to retain the right to get rid of them quickly, you should incorporate a pay in lieu of notice (PILON) clause into your employment contracts. This will allow you to dismiss them immediately providing that you pay them what they would have earned had they worked their full notice period.

EMPLOYER TIP

If you dismiss with insufficient notice, the employee will be able to avoid any obligations you have placed on them under restrictive covenants. This is because you will have breached the contract, and doing so can release the employee from having to perform these obligations.

Another advantage of having a PILON clause is that with some careful drafting you can retain the right to pay an employee basic salary only. You can expressly state that payment in lieu of notice will not include any bonus or commission payment, or any benefit that the employee would otherwise be entitled to during the period for which the payment in lieu is made for.

Download Zone

For a **Pay in Lieu of Notice Clause**, visit **http://books.indicator.co.uk**. You'll find the access code on page 2 of this book.

EMPLOYER TIP 1

You should closely monitor any new employee during their first four weeks with you. Then, if you see a problem emerging, you can either try to salvage the situation, or dismiss them. Do be aware that this is a safe bet only if your reason for dismissal doesn't fall within any of the categories of automatically unfair dismissal, such as discrimination on a protected ground.

EMPLOYER TIP 2

If an employee has committed an act of gross misconduct, you can dismiss without notice, but play it safe and do make staff aware of what behaviour constitutes gross misconduct.

Download Zone

For a **Sample List of Gross Misconduct Offences**, visit **http://books.indicator. co.uk**. You'll find the access code on page 2 of this book.

KEY POINTS

After one month of employment, new employees are entitled to:

- guarantee payments during lay-off or short time working
- full pay during a period of suspension on medical grounds; this is not the same as being "signed off" sick by a medical practitioner
- a minimum of one week's notice.

Breaches can result in:

- a tribunal claim for an unpaid guarantee payment of up to £21.20 per day for up to five days in any three-month period
- a tribunal claim for up to 26 weeks' pay to represent a medical suspension payment
- unlimited compensation for breach of contract.

CHAPTER 4

After eight weeks of employment

4.1. WRITTEN STATEMENT

After eight weeks of employment, employees are entitled to receive what's known as a "written statement of employment particulars". This is not a contract of employment but instead covers all the key details that an employee must be given by law. A separate contract can be given incorporating all the information that must be given in the written statement.

4.1.1. Right to receive a written statement of employment particulars

What's the risk?

Compensation of between two (up to £760) and four weeks' pay (up to £1,520).

If you don't issue a written statement within eight weeks of an employee starting a job, they may be entitled to compensation. This will be based on between two and four times one week's pay (capped at the current statutory rate of £380 a week). However, this type of claim can't be for a standalone action; it must be as part of other proceedings before the tribunal, e.g. a discrimination claim. Neither will it apply if employment continues for less than one month.

How does it work?

If you're going to recruit an employee for one month or more, s.1 of the **Employment Rights Act 1996** requires you to provide them with a written statement of employment particulars. Its purpose is to codify the key terms and conditions that exist between you. It must include the following:

- your company name
- the employee's job title
- date that employment commenced
- date on which the employee's period of continuous employment began
- salary details
- frequency of payment
- hours of work
- holiday entitlement
- sick pay provision, e.g. occupational sick pay or SSP
- pension scheme details
- relevant notice period; and
- the duration of the contract.

In addition to these, you can also add in terms as appropriate. For example, if you're recruiting for a fixed-term contract, you can specify how long the contract is expected to last. However, a written statement doesn't need to be provided if you're going to issue the employee with a full contract of employment.

How to avoid it?

You can avoid any problems by ensuring that you always issue a written statement within eight weeks of a new employee starting work with you. This is much easier than hoping that an employee will not have cause to take you to tribunal for another employment-related matter. In order to satisfy yourself that the written statement has been brought to the employee's attention, you should issue an original and a copy with a covering letter. This should ask the employee to sign the original and return it to you. You should check the content of these statements regularly and update them as necessary.

Download Zone

For a **Written Statement of Employment Particulars**, visit **http://books.indicator. co.uk.** You'll find the access code on page 2 of this book.

KEY POINTS

After eight weeks, new employees are entitled to:
- a written statement of employment particulars.

Failure to provide a statement could result in:
- compensation of between two (capped at £760) and four weeks' pay (capped at £1,520).

CHAPTER 5

At six months

5.1. FAMILY-FRIENDLY RIGHTS

After six months' continuous employment, employees accrue further rights. These can broadly be categorised as "family friendly" as they include the statutory right to request flexible working in connection with caring responsibilities, e.g. children and elderly relatives. However, they also encompass the right to receive statutory maternity pay as well as leave with pay for those who are adopting or are wishing to take paternity leave.

5.1.1. Denial of the right to request flexible working

What's the risk?

Compensation of up to eight weeks' pay at a rate of £380 per week.

Tribunal order for you to reconsider the flexible working request.

Possible sex discrimination claim with unlimited compensation.

The entitlement to compensation is triggered if you fail to: **(1)** consider an employee's request to work flexibly; **(2)** hold a meeting to discuss it; or **(3)** give reasons for refusing a request. The amount deemed to be a week's pay is not the employee's actual salary, but is instead set by statute at £380 per week (currently), meaning that an employee could be awarded up to £3,040 in compensation, but less if they earn only the National Minimum Wage.

No complaint can be brought by an employee until you are in breach of the statutory procedure. Neither can they complain if they have withdrawn their flexible working request. Any tribunal claim must be submitted within three months of the alleged breach occurring and can only be made on the following grounds: **(1)** that you have not followed the correct procedure, such as failing to hold a meeting to discuss the request; **(2)** that you have refused the application for a reason that is not one of the seven accepted reasons for doing so (see below); or **(3)** that your grounds for refusal were based on incorrect facts.

Note. A tribunal can require you to reconsider the flexible working application, but it can't insist that you agree to it.

Also, if you rejected an application made by a female employee she could bring a claim for indirect sex discrimination which, if successful, could lead to an uncapped award. This is because women still have more childcare responsibilities than men, so any insistence from you that a woman with care responsibilities works inflexible hours could be negatively construed. In addition, this would allow the woman involved to challenge the reasons that you gave for refusal.

How does it work?

All carers and parents of children aged under 17 (or under 18 for parents of disabled children) have the right to make a flexible working request. Carers can also make such a request in order to care for an adult who is: **(1)** married to, or the partner or civil partner of, the employee; **(2)** a near relative of the employee; or **(3)** falls into neither category but lives at the same address as the employee. Do note that the definition of a "near relative" is very wide as it also includes adult children and step-relatives. The employee's application must specify the following:

- that the request being made is the right to request to work flexibly
- how the employee meets the eligibility criteria of service, parenthood or caring
- the change requested and the date that the employee would like it to become effective
- the impact that this change may have on you and how any problems may be overcome.

Employer tip

Only one application can be made in any twelve-month period. So if the employee makes a request to look after a dependant child, they can't make another request to care for an adult until the twelve months has expired. However, you are free to allow employees to make more frequent applications.

After receiving the request you have 28 days in which to agree or meet with the employee to discuss it. If you accept the request, you need to confirm this in writing, setting out the date from when the change will become effective. As this will represent a change to the employee's contract, this will need updating to reflect this.

Note. If, however, the request is one that is based on caring for a terminally ill relative, guidance suggests that you can agree a change informally.

Irrespective of the outcome, you must inform the employee in writing within 14 days of the meeting. If the employee is unhappy with your decision, they have a right to appeal within 14 days of receiving it. This must be done in writing and must state the grounds of the appeal. Another meeting must be held and the outcome again communicated to the employee within a further 14 days.

Employer tip

An employee is entitled to be represented at the meeting, but only by a work colleague.

Download Zone

For a **Flexible Working Acceptance Letter**, visit **http://books.indicator.co.uk**. You'll find the access code on page 2 of this book.

How to avoid it?

You can reject any requests that aren't financially viable on one (or more) business-related grounds. These are as follows:

- the burden of additional costs

- a detrimental effect on your ability to meet customer demand

- an inability to recruit extra staff to cover for the employee

- an inability to reorganise work amongst existing staff

- a detrimental impact on quality or performance

- not fitting in with planned structural changes to your business

- there will be insufficient work available at the times when the employee proposes to work.

EMPLOYER TIP

Don't waste time on finding reasons to reject requests that will have very little impact on you. Instead, concentrate on those that will really affect you financially.

Furthermore, you can't reject a request simply by stating that it would be "inconvenient" or "too costly to implement". Instead, you will need evidence as to why it's unacceptable. In order to achieve this, you must always link your reasoning to one or more of the statutory grounds for refusal and nothing else. For example, you mustn't make it obvious that the refusal is connected to the employee's pregnancy or maternity leave itself. Instead, go straight for the business arguments.

EMPLOYER TIP

The most likely scenario you will face is a request to work part-time. Depending on the hours, this could have a major impact on your business. Therefore, concentrate on showing how you will have problems meeting customer demand and re-organising work amongst existing staff.

If your employee suggests a job-share, you can counter this by showing how you will face proportionately higher costs; you'll need to allow for two lots of benefit packages. Plus, you'll need to factor in extra time for a weekly face-to-face handover. There could be two lots of training and development costs to consider too. For complex and specialist jobs, this could add up, so do the sums and let the employee see them. Always remember, the more evidence you have, the easier it will be to justify any rejection.

EMPLOYER TIP 1

If you've rejected one request, you may be able to re-use some of the information gathered to reject any requests made by other employees.

EMPLOYER TIP 2

If an employee won't accept your rejection of their request, consider third-party mediation or conciliation, e.g. through ACAS. It's cheaper than a claim.

Download Zone

For a **Flexible Working Rejection Letter**, visit **http://books.indicator.co.uk**. You'll find the access code on page 2 of this book.

Another problem that you might face is if you've entered into a flexible working arrangement with an employee and unforeseen circumstances mean that you need to revoke it. Whilst the law sets the employee's rights with regards to making and rejecting flexible working requests, no legal provision is made regarding what happens should you need to revoke the agreement. Instead, the matter becomes contractual because the original agreement for flexible working is likely to have become a permanent change to the employee's terms and conditions.

Therefore, you will need to proceed very carefully:

Step 1. Review position. Think carefully about your reasons for needing to revoke the arrangement and consider whether there are any other means of resolving the situation.

Step 2. Get the evidence. If it's unavoidable, ensure that you have evidence that clearly shows: **(1)** what has changed that now requires the employee to attend work on their original terms and conditions; **(2)** why it affects this particular employee; and **(3)** why there's no viable alternative, e.g. the re-allocation of duties or by taking on a part-timer. Go back to the statutory grounds for refusal to back up your argument here.

Step 3. Meeting. Next, meet with the employee concerned; give them a chance to provide their views and listen to any proposals that you may not have considered. Ideally, they will accept the revocation or you can negotiate a compromise based on a new solution. If the employee refuses to accept the need for contractual change, you will have little option but to dismiss on the grounds of "some other substantial reason".

Step 4. Notice. You need to give a reasonable period of notice, which may vary depending on the impact that the revocation will have on the employee. Play it safe and give a minimum of three months' notice of the contractual change taking effect.

EMPLOYER TIP

Retain the contractual right to revoke a flexible working arrangement in certain circumstances.

Example

"In exceptional circumstances, we may need to alter or revoke a flexible working agreement. This will only occur where circumstances outside our control mean that, for business reasons, its continuation is no longer feasible. If this happens, we will meet with you to explore other options. However, the needs of the Company must take priority."

Download Zone

For a **Flexible Working Policy**, visit **http://books.indicator.co.uk**. You'll find the access code on page 2 of this book.

5.1.2. Right to statutory maternity pay (SMP)

What's the risk?

Complaint to HMRC and a fine of up to £3,000 for each refusal/failure to pay SMP.

Possible sex discrimination claim with unlimited compensation.

Although a failure to pay SMP is unlikely, it does occur. In most cases it's due to a misunderstanding as to entitlement and when it's triggered. Should this happen, the employee may complain to HMRC. It will then investigate and has the power to impose a fine of £3,000 for each employee that you fail to pay.

Note. The actual penalty is based on the total amount of incorrect payments made and/or how often the offence of failing to pay SMP has been committed. Another potential, and far more costly, claim an employee could make is one of sex discrimination.

How does it work?

In order to qualify for SMP, the employee must:

- have worked for you continuously for at least 26 weeks by the notification week, e.g. the end of the 15th week before the estimated week of childbirth
- earn weekly average earnings that are at least equal to the lower earnings limit for NI contributions, e.g. earnings of at least £97 per week
- have complied with notification requirements
- continue to be employed up to the start of the notification week.

Assuming the employee qualifies, she is entitled to receive SMP for up to 39 weeks (depending on how much of this period she chooses to spend on maternity leave). For the first six weeks, this is paid at the "higher rate" which is 90% of the employee's average gross weekly earnings. For the remaining weeks, it's paid at the "lower rate" which is either 90% of gross weekly earnings or at the statutory rate of £124.88 per week; whichever is lower.

The earliest that an employee can start receiving SMP is the 11th week before the baby is due and the latest is the week after the baby is born. Unless the employee is off sick, she can decide when she wishes SMP to start. However, if she is sick with a pregnancy-related illness in the four weeks before her baby is due, SMP will start immediately. If it is a non-pregnancy-related illness, the employee can either claim SSP or occupational sick pay (if she's entitled to it) until the week that the baby is due.

Note. If your Class 1 National Insurance contributions (NICs) are £45,000 or less, you can claim back all the SMP that you have paid plus 4.5% compensation (taking it to 104.5%). However, if your Class 1 NICs are more than £45,000, you can only claim back 92% of the SMP paid. More information can be found at: **http://www. hmrc.gov.uk/employers/recover-smp.htm**.

EMPLOYER TIP

If paying SMP is likely to cause you cash flow problems, contact the HMRC helpline on 08457 143 143, as you may be eligible to claim the money in advance.

How to avoid it?

Apart from familiarising yourself with how SMP works, you can avoid problems by ensuring that you understand what information you are entitled to receive as evidence of an employee's pregnancy. Whilst medical evidence is usually via a MATB1 Maternity Certificate, you can accept any document that has been signed by a doctor or midwife, providing that it includes the date the baby is due. If the original certificate has been lost, you can accept a duplicate copy that has been based on the original medical examination as long as it's marked as a duplicate.

Note. More information can be found by downloading a free leaflet: *"Employer Helpbook for Statutory Maternity Pay - to use for employees whose babies are due on or after 4 April 2010"*, from **http://www/hmrc.gov.uk/helpsheets/e15.pdf**.

Download Zone

For a **Maternity Policy**, visit **http://books.indicator.co.uk**. You'll find the access code on page 2 of this book.

5.1.3.   Right to statutory paternity pay (SPP) and leave

What's the risk?

Complaint to HMRC and a fine of up to £3,000 for each refusal/failure to pay SPP.

Tribunal complaint of detriment arising from refusal to give leave with potentially unlimited compensation.

If you don't pay an employee the SPP that they're entitled to, they may complain to HMRC. It will investigate and can fine you up to £3,000 for each employee that you fail to pay. The actual penalty is based on the total amount of incorrect payments made and how often the offence of failing to pay SPP has been committed. Equally, if you subject the employee to a detriment for insisting on their statutory right to take both SPP and leave, they can bring a tribunal claim and be awarded compensation that is "just and equitable" in the circumstances. This is potentially unlimited.

How does it work?

Fathers and the partner of the mother in a same-sex relationship have a statutory right to take two weeks' paid paternity leave, currently paid at the rate of £124.88 a week. This is to allow them to provide support to their wives and partners around the time of their child's birth. Although the government originally estimated that there would be 450,000 individuals eligible each year to take up this statutory right, few have actually done so. In fact, according to research, only 2.7% of men have taken paternity leave over a two-year period due to the poor pay.

Note. The principles of SPP are similar to SMP. Therefore, the amount recoverable by you as an employer is dependent on the total gross amount of employer and employee Class 1 NICs you have paid in the appropriate tax year.

The poor take-up of SPP has led to the introduction of the **Additional Paternity Leave Regulations 2010** and the **Additional Statutory Paternity Pay (General) Regulations 2010**. Although these Regulations came into force on April 6 2010, they will only apply in respect of babies due on or after April 3 2011. Under these Regulations, eligible fathers and partners (including women in same-sex relationships), will be able to take up to 26 weeks' additional paternity leave to care for the child. However, the mother must have returned to work with enough of her 52-week maternity leave remaining. Therefore, the new entitlement will only be up to the point when the mother's statutory maternity leave would have ended.

So if a man takes over at 26 weeks, he will be entitled to paternity pay for 13 weeks followed by unpaid leave for 13 weeks. On today's figures, this means that he would be paid £124.88 per week or 90% of his salary, whichever is lower. In practice, take-up of this extension is likely to be poor as most men won't be able to afford such a drop in salary, particularly if they earn more than their spouse/partner.

How to avoid it?

Although it's unlikely that an employee will apply for paternity leave (they're more likely to take annual leave), you should be prepared. This means checking eligibility in order to avoid getting caught out. You can do this by ensuring that the employee making the request:

- has worked for you for at least 26 weeks by the notification week, e.g. the end of the 15th week before the EWC
- has or expects to have responsibility for bringing up the child
- is the biological father or married to, or the civil partner or the partner of, the child's mother; and
- earns more than the Lower Earnings Limit for NI contributions (currently £97 per week). Fathers or partners who earn less than this can still take leave but they have no statutory right to be paid.

An employee may take either one or two weeks' paternity leave. The leave can't be taken as odd days and if an employee wishes to take two weeks, they must be taken together. This will make it easier and less time consuming for you to administer. This entitlement could be set out in a paternity leave policy. Any policy should make it clear that you have the right to ask them to sign a self-certificate that will: **(1)** describe the nature of their relationship to the child's mother; **(2)** confirm that they have (or expect to have) responsibility for the child's upbringing; and **(3)** confirm that the purpose of their application for paternity leave is to support the child's mother.

Note. If you don't do this now, it will certainly become necessary in April 2011 when employees may wish to avail themselves of the new right to take additional paternity leave. You should also be aware that in nearly all cases, an employee taking this leave has the right to return to the job that they were doing immediately before leave commenced.

Download Zone

For a **Paternity Leave Policy**, visit **http://books.indicator.co.uk**. You'll find the access code on page 2 of this book.

5.1.4.   Right to statutory adoption pay (SAP) and leave

What's the risk?

Complaint to HMRC and a fine of up to £3,000 for each refusal/failure to pay SAP.

Tribunal complaint of detriment arising from refusal to give leave with potentially unlimited compensation.

If you don't pay an employee the SAP that they are entitled to, they can complain to HMRC. It will investigate and could fine you up to £3,000 for this failure. In the unlikely event that more than one employee is adopting, this penalty could be levied for each refusal of SAP that you make. The actual penalty is based on the total amount of incorrect payments made and/or how often the offence of failing to pay SAP has been committed. Equally, if you subject the employee to a detriment for insisting on their statutory right to take this leave, they can bring a tribunal claim and be awarded compensation that is "just and equitable". This is potentially unlimited.

How does it work?

Employees who qualify and wish to take this leave are protected from suffering any detriment and are also protected from unfair dismissal. The first six months of adoption leave is known as ordinary adoption leave (OAL) with the second six months referred to as additional adoption leave (AAL). In terms of adoption pay, there are two types. By far the most common is SAP which is payable for up to 39 weeks at a rate of £124.88 (or at 90% of average earnings if earning less than this). Alternatively, you may offer enhanced company adoption pay. This is more likely to be the case if you already offer an equivalent package for maternity pay. Once an employee applies for adoption leave, you have 28 days in which to acknowledge the request and inform the employee of the date on which they are due to return to work after taking the leave.

SAP works in a similar way to maternity pay. This means that the employee will still be entitled to receive any commission or bonus payments relating to work carried out before the start of OAL. So make a note that they will need to receive any pro rata payment that's due whilst on leave. SAP can be reclaimed in the same way (and following the same principles) as SMP. You should be aware that an employee will still be legally entitled to receive contractual benefits except remuneration during OAL and AAL. You also need to be aware that in nearly all cases, an employee returning to work from taking adoption leave is entitled to return to their old job.

Note. As with paternity leave, the same legal changes that were introduced on April 6 2010 will come into force on April 3 2011, providing that the adopter is notified of a match for adoption on or after this date. This means that providing the primary adopter returns to work, the father or same sex partner can have the remainder of the leave transferred to them.

EMPLOYER TIP

There's no legal requirement for you to pay over and above the statutory amount - so no requirement for any company adoption pay.

How to avoid it?

Even though the rights of adopters have been strengthened in recent years, not all employees will be entitled to statutory adoption leave. So if one of your employees decides to adopt, check that they qualify for SAP. In order to do so, the employee must:

- be newly matched with a child for adoption by an approved adoption agency, formally becoming a step-parent of a partner's child doesn't qualify

- be the primary carer of the child

- have 26 weeks' continuous service with you by the week they are notified of being matched with a child for adoption

- earn more than the Lower Earnings Limit for NI contributions (currently £97 per week).

If the employee fulfils these criteria, you can't refuse to allow them the time off. Neither can you discriminate against them because of it. This is likely to lead to a costly claim for sex discrimination because those taking adoption leave still tend to be female. This is a good argument for having an adoption leave policy as it can set out the legal position clearly.

EMPLOYER TIP

For the avoidance of doubt, ask to see a Matching Certificate as evidence of the adoption.

Download Zone

For an **Adoption Leave and Pay Policy**, visit **http://books.indicator.co.uk**. You'll find the access code on page 2 of this book.

KEY POINTS

After six months, new employees have the right to:

- request to work flexibly
- receive statutory maternity pay (SMP)
- receive statutory paternity pay (SPP) and leave
- receive statutory adoption pay (SAP) and leave.

Failure to comply can lead to:

- up to eight weeks' pay (at currently £380 per week) for failure to consider a flexible working request
- a tribunal order for you to reconsider a particular flexible working request
- a possible sex discrimination claim for refusal to consider a flexible working request
- a complaint to the HMRC and a fine of up to £3,000 for each refusal/failure to pay SMP, SPP and SAP
- just and equitable compensation for suffering detriment connected with requesting SPP or SAP.

CHAPTER 6

At one year

6.1. UNFAIR DISMISSAL

Once an employee has attained one complete year of continuous employment with you, they gain protection against unfair dismissal. Also, they're entitled to be given written reasons for any such dismissal.

6.1.1. The right not to be unfairly dismissed and to receive written reasons for dismissal

What's the risk?

A maximum award of £76,700 (comprised of a basic award of up to £11,400 and a compensatory award of up to £65,300).

Compensation can be increased (or reduced) by 25% where the ACAS code is breached.

A tribunal order to reinstate or re-engage the employee.

An additional award may be made where an order for re-instatement or re-engagement is made but not complied with. If this applies, this extra award will be between £9,880 and £19,760.

Two weeks' actual pay for failure to provide written reasons for dismissal.

An unfair dismissal claim is most likely to occur if an employee alleges that you haven't followed a fair disciplinary and dismissal process, or if you have tried to dismiss without taking into account the relevant notice period that would take them into a full year's employment with you. If the employee is successful, any tribunal award received will comprise of a basic award and possibly an extra compensatory award. The basic award is calculated on the same basis as a statutory redundancy payment, so the amount used for weekly pay won't exceed £380. The second award is a compensatory element. Its exact amount will be what a tribunal decides is "just and equitable" in the circumstances. In deciding what award to make, the tribunal will need to look at the loss sustained by the employee as a result of the dismissal, insofar as that loss is attributable to your actions as the employer.

The compensatory award is meant to cover any loss of wages and fringe benefits from the point of dismissal. However, it will be reduced if the dismissed employee has found new work. Orders of re-instatement and re-engagement are very unusual, but if you fail to comply with any order made, the tribunal can add on an extra penalty. Again, this award is based on the statutory amount of a week's pay (£380) and will vary from between 26 and 52 weeks' pay. In addition, the tribunal can increase or reduce compensation by up to 25% if you (or the employee) fail to follow the ACAS Code of Practice on Disciplinary and Grievance Procedures. The employee is also entitled to receive written reasons for their dismissal. Any failure to provide them, i.e. if you fail to respond to an employee's request within 14 days of receiving it, will lead to a tribunal awarding the employee two weeks' actual pay in compensation.

How does it work?

The basic award is calculated as follows:

(Age factor) x (length of service) x (week's pay capped at £380)

An employee is entitled to receive half a week's pay for each complete year of employment where they are under the age of 22, one week's pay for each complete year of employment between the ages of 22 and 40 and one and a half weeks' pay for each complete year of employment if aged 41 or over. In terms of length of service, up to 20 years is the maximum and this is counted backwards starting from the employee's date of termination.

> *Example*
>
> *Helen has been unfairly dismissed from ABC Ltd. She is 30 years old and has worked for it for ten full years. So her basic tribunal award would be:*
>
> *(1 x 8 x £380) + (0.5 x 2 x £380) = £3,420 plus any compensatory award*

The compensatory element of any award isn't mandatory, so might not be made. Equally, an award can be reduced to reflect certain circumstances. For example, the tribunal may do this where the employee contributed to their dismissal or where they failed to mitigate their financial loss, i.e. did not look for a new job. However, in poor economic conditions, a tribunal is less likely to penalise an ex-employee for not finding new employment, though they will still be expected to produce evidence of any attempts made.

How to avoid it?

You can reduce the likelihood of an unfair dismissal claim by working through the following steps:

Step 1. Establish the facts. Investigate disciplinary matters without "unreasonable delay". The ACAS Code states that if misconduct is involved, then the investigation and disciplinary hearing "should" be carried out by different people. However, it's acknowledged that this may not always be possible for small businesses. Whatever you do, don't allow any investigatory meeting to accidentally turn into a disciplinary hearing. The same principle applies to any meeting during which an employee is suspended as part of the investigation.

Step 2. Notify the employee. If the investigation shows that a disciplinary hearing is justified, notify the employee in writing and include the following information: **(1)** the reasons why your disciplinary proceedings have been invoked; **(2)** the possible consequences for the employee, e.g. dismissal; **(3)** copies of any written evidence, e.g. witness statements; **(4)** a reminder to the employee of their right to be accompanied; and **(5)** the date and time of the hearing.

Step 3. The hearing. The Code provides that whilst the employee should have reasonable time to prepare their case, the hearing should be held without unreasonable delay. Where the sanction is likely to be dismissal, it's particularly important to allow the employee enough time to prepare any defence. The Code also states that if an employee is *"persistently unable or unwilling to attend a disciplinary meeting without good cause..."*, that you can proceed without them being present. Should an employee suspect that they are going to be dismissed, they might try to delay matters by not turning up. Unfortunately, no assistance is given in the Code as to what counts as "persistent". Until this is clarified by the Employment Appeal Tribunal, we would advise that you consider defining two no-shows as persistent. The format of the meeting remains unchanged from the old statutory regime, so start by setting out the nature of the complaint and outline your evidence. Give the employee plenty of opportunity to put their case and respond to any allegations (even more important when dismissal is likely).

Step 4. Statutory right to be accompanied. The old statutory right to be accompanied at a disciplinary meeting has transferred to the new regime. So as before, the chosen companion must be either a colleague, trade union representative, or an official employed by a trade union.

Step 5. Action to take. After the meeting you must inform the employee in writing of the outcome. For dismissal, the Code provides that the decision should only be taken by a manager who has the express authority to dismiss.

EMPLOYER TIP

Always remind the employee of their right to appeal, but avoid any uncertainty by setting out the deadline for this.

Step 6. Right of appeal. If an employee wishes to appeal, they should let you know their grounds in writing. Should an appeal be made, you're required to deal with it impartially and without unreasonable delay. Ideally, it should be heard by a manager who hasn't had any previous involvement in the case. The statutory right to be accompanied still applies. Once it has taken place, you should inform the employee of the outcome in writing and promptly.

Don't be tempted to just pay lip service to the appeal process. This is because it's your last chance to show the employee that you care and to ensure that the process has been reasonable in all the circumstances. If you give the impression that you're rushing to get it over and done with, the employee is more likely to punish you by taking you to tribunal.

Note. You do need to watch notice periods. If poor performance or poor attitude is allowed to continue during an employee's first year, the employee may be close to accruing one year's continuous employment. You can do much to avoid this by monitoring an employee closely during their probation. By doing this, you can pick up any problems and give them chance to improve without being at risk of them accruing a full year's service.

Download Zone

For a **Disciplinary Procedure**, visit **http://books.indicator.co.uk**. You'll find the access code on page 2 of this book.

6.2. FAMILY-FRIENDLY

In terms of family-friendly rights, the one-year mark is when an employee finally becomes eligible to exercise their right to take parental leave.

6.2.1. Right to take parental leave

What's the risk?

Tribunal declaration that refusal to grant parental leave was unlawful.

Complaint of detriment arising from this refusal with potentially unlimited compensation.

If you deny an employee the right to take parental leave, they can complain to a tribunal and ask for a declaration that your refusal was unlawful. The tribunal may also order that you pay compensation for subjecting the employee to a detriment. Such an award carries potentially unlimited compensation as it will be based on an amount that the tribunal believes reflects the loss suffered.

How does it work?

Parental leave provides parents with the right to take one or more periods of unpaid leave from work to look after a child, or to make arrangements for a child's welfare. Both mothers and fathers are eligible to take it providing its purpose is to genuinely care for a child. Its purpose is to be an extra source of leave that can be called upon to help achieve a better work-life balance. Same-sex parents are covered as well as adoptive parents.

Unless the child is disabled, parental leave can be taken for up to 13 weeks per child in blocks of up to four weeks at a time. Whilst it's unlikely to be practical for a small business, you can agree to allow an employee to take more than four weeks' leave in one go. A qualifying employee must give you at least 21 days' notice of their intention to take parental leave and you should insist that this is given in writing.

Note. More information entitled "Parental leave: a guide for employers and employees" can be downloaded from **http://www.workingbalance.co.uk/pdf/parental.pdf**.

EMPLOYER TIP

You have the right to postpone the commencement of parental leave for up to six months if it would cause your business undue disruption. However, you would need to show evidence of this.

How to avoid it?

In order to avoid unnecessary misunderstandings and conflict, you should be aware of who is and isn't eligible to apply for parental leave. Currently, to qualify, an employee must:

- have one year's qualifying service at the time that they wish to take leave
- have or expect to have responsibility for a child. You can ask for proof of this
- be the parent of a baby or child born or adopted on or after December 15 1999.

The definition of parent includes adoptive parents, same-sex couples or the new partner of a parent. So don't risk a time-consuming grievance or a costly discrimination claim by trying to exclude any qualifying employee that belongs to one of these categories. Also note that if your employee has a child that qualifies for disabled living allowance, they can take leave in blocks or multiples of one day. Otherwise, the law provides that parental leave can only be taken in minimum blocks of one week. The advantage of this is that you don't have to worry about keeping records of odd days taken here and there.

Note. At the end of parental leave, the employee has a right to return to the same job and on the same terms and conditions, providing that the leave period was for no more than a four-week block. If leave was taken for longer than this, then the employee doesn't have the right to return to the same job (if not reasonably practicable to do so), but is entitled to a suitable alternative. This must be one that offers matching or improved terms and conditions.

If the employee's proposal to take parental leave would be disruptive to your business and you need to postpone it, you'll need clear evidence why. In practice, this not only requires you to show how the employee is critical to your business, but also how they are essential at this particular time, e.g. seasonal peaks and troughs. Should a need to postpone apply, you will need to discuss this with the employee and see if there are reasonable alternatives. If not, you should write to them no later than seven days from receipt of the request to take this leave. Your letter should detail the reason(s) for the postponement.

EMPLOYER TIP

Do note that leave can't be postponed if an application for parental leave is made by an employee to take immediately after a child is born or placed for adoption, providing the employee complies with the 21-day notice period requirements.

Download Zone

For a **Parental Leave Policy**, visit **http://books.indicator.co.uk**. You'll find the access code on page 2 of this book.

Download Zone

For a **Refusal of a Parental Leave Request**, visit **http://books.indicator.co.uk**. You'll find the access code on page 2 of this book.

KEY POINTS

After one year of employment, employees are entitled to:

- not be unfairly dismissed
- receive written reasons for dismissal
- take parental leave in minimum blocks of one week.

Breaches can result in:

- a maximum award of £76,700 (comprised of a basic award of up to £11,400 and a compensatory award of £65,300)
- compensation being increased (or reduced) by 25% if you breach the ACAS code
- a tribunal order to reinstate or re-engage the employee
- an extra award being made if you don't comply with an order to re-instate or re-engage
- two weeks' actual pay for failure to provide written reasons for dismissal
- a tribunal declaration that refusal to grant parental leave was unlawful
- a potentially unlimited compensation award for failure to grant parental leave.

CHAPTER 7

At two years

7.1.   REDUNDANCY

Once an employee has two years' continuous employment with you, more legal rights come their way. The main ones are that they become entitled to receive a statutory redundancy payment and to have reasonable time off to look for work once they are under a notice of redundancy.

7.1.1.   The right to receive a statutory redundancy payment, time off to look for work and consultation over collective redundancies

How does it work?

What's the risk?

Tribunal claim for compensation equal to the amount of statutory redundancy payment (SRP) owed.

Tribunal claim for compensation for failure to be given time off to look for work (40% of a week's pay).

A protective award that could be up to 90 days' full pay.

If an employee being made redundant fulfils the two-year criterion, they are entitled to receive an SRP. If you fail to pay this within six months, or pay the incorrect amount, they can apply to a tribunal for an order forcing you to pay it on the basis that you have made an unlawful deduction from wages. They have up to six months after the money becomes due to make a claim.

Equally, if you deny an employee their statutory right to take reasonable time off to look for alternative work, they can issue a tribunal claim to enforce this right. This award is currently set at 40%, or two-fifths, of a week's pay.

In the event that you are dealing with what's known as a collective redundancy situation, where 20 or more redundancies become necessary at one establishment within a period of 90 days, the process of "collective" consultation is triggered. If you fail to consult with appropriate representatives, such as those from one or more recognised trade unions, a tribunal can make a "protective" award. This could prove very expensive, as it could be equivalent to up to 90 days' actual pay for each employee that you have dismissed or whom you propose to dismiss as redundant.

How does it work?

As well as having two years' continuous service, the employee must not have unreasonably refused to accept alternative employment. However, there are a few types of employee that don't qualify for an SRP, such as apprentices. If an employee does qualify, they're entitled to a tax-free lump sum that is calculated according to: **(1)** age; **(2)** length of service; and **(3)** gross weekly wage. The current weekly limit for SRP is £380.

Note. Under the **Employment Equality (Age) Regulations 2006**, the minimum age of 18 and maximum age of 65 was abolished. However, the age factor used to calculate the multiplier still applies. This is because evidence shows that older employees find it harder to obtain new work following redundancy. Therefore the multiplier works as follows:

For each complete year of service up to a maximum of 20, employees are entitled to:

- Half a week's pay for each year of service under the age of 22.

- One week's pay for each year of service at age 22 to 40.

- One and a half weeks' pay for each year of service at age 41 or over.

For legal purposes, the word "redundancy" has a very specific meaning. Under s.139(1) of the **Employment Relations Act 1999**, it's defined as where an employee's dismissal is wholly or mainly due to the fact that: **(1)** the business is closing; **(2)** the particular workplace (or site) where an employee is based is closing; **(3)** there is, or will be, a diminishing requirement for employees to carry out work of a particular type; or **(4)** a diminishing requirement for employees to carry out work of a particular type at the place where an employee is employed. Redundancy is therefore a very specific reason for dismissal and is one of the categories under which a dismissal may be potentially fair.

Those facing redundancy are entitled to reasonable time off to attend job interviews or to arrange training. The law deliberately doesn't define what's "reasonable" as this will vary from employee to employee and will arguably depend on the ease of finding alternative employment in a particular region. Irrespective of this, the amount of time off must be agreed before the period of notice expires. You're only obliged to pay two-fifths of a week's pay (40%), regardless of the amount of time you allow an employee to have off to look for a new job. This right only applies to those who are entitled to receive SRP, and the sum is calculated by dividing a week's pay by the number of normal working hours in the week. Employees are also entitled to reasonable time off to attend job interviews or to arrange training. You are free to offer more than this and many employers will pay full salary.

If collective consultation has been triggered, you should be aware of the legal requirements you must comply with in order to avoid the risk of having to pay a "protective award". If you recognise trade unions, this consultation will be carried out with their representatives. If you don't recognise, you'll need to consult with any staff representatives that exist under the **Information and Consultation of Employees Regulations 2004** (ICER). These Regulations apply if you have at least 50 employees. If you don't have any formal arrangements in place - either because ICER don't apply or because employees haven't previously requested that arrangements be set up - it's your responsibility to rectify this. Should 10% of your workforce make a request (or at least 15 employees), ICER provide that employee representatives must be appointed or elected within three months.

How to avoid it?

In terms of SRP, you can avoid a claim by ensuring that you understand the rules on entitlement and how it's calculated. You should pay the employee on, or as soon as possible after, their departure and include a letter that shows exactly how the redundancy payment has been calculated.

Download Zone

For a **Redundancy Payments Ready Reckoner**, visit **http://books.indicator.co.uk**. You'll find the access code on page 2 of this book.

EMPLOYER TIP

Don't allow redundancy consultation to continue excessively as it could push qualifying employees into another year's service for pay calculations.

When dealing with the right to time off to look for work, your obligation is only triggered once you reach the formal redundancy notice period. If you have just given advance warning that redundancies are likely, an employee has no right to time off at that stage. Should one or more employees wish to take time off to look for a new job at this point, they can take annual leave. You also have the right to see evidence that any leave taken is used to look for work. This means that you can ask to see letters offering the employee an interview. Equally, if the employee wants to use the time off to look at undertaking further training or re-training, you can ask for evidence of a college open day etc.

You also need to be careful when dealing with consultation. Many employers still don't understand that consultation refers to meaningful two-way dialogue. Merely notifying employees that redundancies are inevitable doesn't comply with your legal duties. If you are non-unionised and are dealing with employee representatives, you have six months following their election to establish how consultation will work. This time-frame emphasises the importance of notifying employees of possible redundancies quickly in order to get formal consultation arrangements set up. However, if your workforce fails to elect representatives, despite being given the opportunity to do so, you can fulfil your legal obligations by providing relevant information to the employees likely to be affected directly.

The duty is to "consult" and have genuine two-way discussions about a redundancy programme; you don't have to reach an agreement.

Note. A single establishment refers to different sites. So if you're planning on making a few employees from each site redundant, but the total number is 20 or more, the collective consultation provisions will still apply. This is a legal requirement which can't be avoided or circumvented in any way.

7.2. NOTICE

In terms of notice periods, employees' rights are extended and they have the statutory right to a minimum of two weeks' notice.

7.2.1. Right to two weeks' minimum notice on the termination of employment

What's the risk?

Unlimited compensation for breach of contract.

If you dismiss an employee with two years' service without giving at least two weeks' notice, they could bring a tribunal claim against you. This would be for breach of contract, and the substance of the claim would be for the employee to be placed in the financial position that they would have been in had you given the notice they were legally entitled to. The amount claimed would generally be for any basic salary owing but not paid and the equivalent of any benefits that they would have enjoyed during the notice period. Any claim is likely to be heard at tribunal as it will doubtless be for far less than the £25,000 maximum.

How does it work?

Once an employee accrues two years' continuous employment, they are entitled to receive a minimum of two weeks' notice if their employment is going to be terminated. An employee with two years' service will also be able to claim for any benefits that they would have enjoyed had they been given the correct notice period.

Note. An employee is entitled to an extra week's notice for every year of service up to twelve years. So if they have eight years' service, they are entitled to receive eight weeks' notice.

How to avoid it?

In practice, you're likely to have longer notice periods, such as one month. However, irrespective of this, you should still incorporate a pay in lieu of notice clause into your employment contracts. This will allow you to dismiss an employee immediately providing that you pay them what they would have earned had they worked their full notice period. If you don't and dismiss with insufficient notice, the risk is that the employee may be able to avoid any obligations that you have incorporated into their employment contract, such as a restrictive covenant. This is because you will have breached the contract and by so doing released the employee from having to perform their contractual obligations.

Download Zone

For a **Pay in Lieu of Notice Clause**, visit **http://books.indicator.co.uk**. You'll find the access code on page 2 of this book.

KEY POINTS

After two years of employment, employees are entitled to:

- receive a statutory redundancy payment (SRP)
- reasonable time off to look for work when under a notice of redundancy
- be consulted over collective redundancies
- a right to two weeks' minimum notice on the termination of employment.

Breaches can result in a:

- tribunal claim for compensation equal to the amount of SRP owing
- tribunal claim for compensation for failure to be given time off to look for work (40% of a week's pay)
- protective award that could be up to 90 days' pay for failure to consult over collective redundancies
- breach of contract claim for failing to give the two weeks' minimum notice.

CHAPTER 8

Post-employment

8.1. REFERENCES

You may think that once an employee leaves, any specific duties you owe them cease to exist. In fact, some will remain. The main one is with regard to any reference that you provide: an employee has the right to a reference that is factually accurate and has been written with due care and attention.

8.1.1. Failure to take reasonable care when writing a reference

What's the risk?

Compensation for breach of contract and/or negligence.

Unlimited compensation for post-employment discrimination.

It's possible for an employee to obtain a copy of any reference that you provided for them by making a "subject access request" under the **Data Protection Act 1998**. If they then found that you had included statements you couldn't back up, e.g. you had erroneously claimed that they had taken far more sick leave than they actually had, or they were very disruptive without any evidence of it, they could attempt to mount a claim against you in the county court. This is most likely to happen where a job offer has been withdrawn as a result of the reference.

If you compiled the reference whilst they were still employed, their claim would be for a breach of an implied contractual term (an employee would only be able to sue you for breach of an express term if the right to a reference was specifically included in your employment contract). An alternative would be for them to allege that you acted negligently and they suffered economic loss as a result of an inaccurate reference, e.g. they lost a substantial pay rise and any benefits offered to join this new employer.

How does it work?

Unless you work in the financial services sector, or your employment contracts provide for the giving of a reference, you are not obliged by law to provide one. However, where you do agree, you're under a duty to take reasonable care so it's factually accurate and fair. The leading case in this area is **Spring v Guardian Assurance plc 1994**. Here it was held that employers owe a duty of care to provide a reference that is *"true, accurate and fair"* which is achieved by exercising *"reasonable care"* in its compilation.

Note. In addition, an employee who is protected from discrimination on the grounds of sex, sexual orientation, race, disability, age, religion or belief could argue that they were a victim of post-employment discrimination on one or more of these grounds. If they pursue this route and are successful, then you are looking at a potentially unlimited compensatory award.

How to avoid it?

In order to avoid problems, you must stick to facts when writing references. So if you are asked to comment on sick leave, or an employee's disciplinary history, check your records before commenting. However, if you feel that the employee is the sort to make real trouble for you, even if they have a disastrous work and sickness absence record, you could simply decline to give a reference. After all, there's usually no obligation on you to give one and equally employees have no right to expect one will be forthcoming.

If you decide on this course of action, you should still acknowledge the reference request and simply state that you are unable to provide a reference.

Download Zone

For a **Letter Declining a Reference**, visit **http://books.indicator.co.uk**. You'll find the access code on page 2 of this book.

Note. The exception is if the employee is leaving under a compromise agreement and it contained a clause that provided for an "agreed reference". If you don't comply, you will be in breach of the terms of the compromise agreement.

EMPLOYER TIP

If you don't want to provide a reference, avoid using the word "unwilling", as it sounds contentious; simply state that you are "unable" to as a matter of company policy.

8.2.   ANNUAL LEAVE

8.2.1.   Payment in lieu for annual leave accrued but not taken

What's the risk?

Compensation representing the value of the untaken leave.

When an employee leaves they are entitled to be paid for any annual leave that they have accrued but not taken. If you fail to compensate for this, they can bring a tribunal claim.

How does it work?

Irrespective of how short the period of employment may be, an employee has the right to be paid for any accrued holiday. This applies to both statutory leave under working time legislation, as well as a more generous contractual entitlement. You also need to be aware of recent case law developments in relation to those on long-term sickness absence: they are now able to accrue statutory annual leave whilst off sick. This means that any employee who has been off sick for several weeks or months and then leaves your employment, e.g. under medical retirement or ill-health dismissal, is entitled to be paid any holiday accrued but not taken.

How to avoid it?

You can avoid problems by paying the soon-to-be ex-employee the exact amount of holiday pay that is owed to them. This can be done by using a formula that involves multiplying the annual leave entitlement by the proportion of leave that has expired and then subtracting the number of days' leave that has already been taken:

A (overall leave entitlement) x B (proportion of leave year that had expired before employment ended) – C (amount of leave already taken before employment ended).

> *Example*
>
> *Kate worked five days a week and was entitled to six weeks' annual leave. Her employment ends after six months. In that leave year she had already taken five days (one week's) leave. So she is owed:*
>
> *6.0 weeks x 0.5 – 1 week = 2 weeks' pay owing*

In the event that the employee has taken proportionately more leave than they are entitled to, you can't deduct the overpayment unless you have retained the contractual right to do so using a holiday pay on termination clause. The employee will have the right to bring an unlawful deduction of wages claim without such a clause.

Download Zone

For a **Holiday Pay on Termination Clause**, visit **http://books.indicator.co.uk**. You'll find the access code on page 2 of this book.

8.3. RESTRICTIVE COVENANTS

Ex-employees have the right not to have any unreasonable restrictions placed upon them post-employment, e.g. via excessively wide restrictive covenants.

8.3.1. Excessive post-employment restrictive covenants

What's the risk?

Potential for the entire clause to be struck out.

If you draft a restrictive covenant that goes further than is necessary to protect your business interests, the risk is that a tribunal will strike out the entire clause, not just the parts that the employee is objecting to. This leaves you vulnerable, as the tribunal won't substitute a more suitable clause for you.

How does it work?

Many employers place restrictive covenants into their employment contracts in order to protect their legitimate business interests. There are different types of post-employment restriction that you may need to implement for a defined time period, e.g. preventing an employee from setting up another company in direct competition, or working for a main competitor and poaching clients, suppliers and key employees. They are particularly useful for controlling the activities of senior and highly specialist employees.

The biggest risk is the departing employee who helps themselves to confidential information on the way out. This could include a variety of "intangible" assets, e.g. customer lists, prototypes of new products, pricing lists, salary structure and other types of business know-how, which are all unique to your business. Reports suggest that employees who are made redundant are more likely to steal sensitive information from an employer because they believe it will give them a head-start in a new job. They may also do it out of resentment. Unfortunately, this type of litigation is both costly and time-consuming. Therefore, you need to take steps to protect yourself from the misuse of confidential business information, but in a way that a tribunal/court won't deem excessive.

How to avoid it?

Taking the following steps will reduce the risk of a tribunal striking out some, or all, of your post-employment restrictions:

Step 1. Identify key information. Begin by identifying all the intangible assets that could jeopardise your business if passed onto a competitor. In addition to data such as customer lists and new designs, also include less obvious information such as any specialist safety management systems and bonus structure that you have in place. Once you've done this you need to include it in your definition of "confidential information". Otherwise, your departing employees won't know what qualifies and what doesn't.

Step 2. Identify classes of employee. Next, find those employees who have access to this information and who could benefit from it should they leave your employment. As a rule of thumb, the more senior the employee, the greater the restrictions that should apply to them.

Step 3. Identify clients. When you're looking at which employees need to be covered, also consider their clients. This is because you could be challenged if you try to enforce a widely drafted clause that purports to ban an employee from poaching any of your clients. Instead, restrict the clause to the employee's own customers. This is likely to apply to senior staff and those developing new products or services. If you want it to have a wider application, be sure that you can justify it.

Step 4. Extent of restriction. Remember that the restrictions must be no wider than is necessary to protect your legitimate business interests. So consider how long the restriction will need to apply post-employment and its geographical extent.

Step 5. Monitor access to key information. Periodically check that employment contracts and job descriptions are updated in line with promotions. This will ensure that contractual obligations match an employee's new status so you won't have any nasty surprises when they leave.

Download Zone

For a **Restrictive Covenants Clause**, visit **http://books.indicator.co.uk**. You'll find the access code on page 2 of this book.

KEY POINTS

Post employment, employees are entitled to:

- receive a reference that has been prepared with due care and skill
- payment in lieu for any accrued but untaken annual leave
- not be subjected to excessive post-employment restrictions.

Any breach could result in:

- compensation for breach of contract or negligence in how you drafted a reference
- unlimited compensation for post-employment discrimination, e.g. on the grounds of race
- compensation representing the value of the employee's outstanding annual leave
- the potential for entire clauses on post-employment restrictions to be struck out.

CHAPTER 9

Documents

ADOPTION LEAVE AND PAY POLICY

The Company implements the adoption leave rights set out in legislation. This section sets out the Company's policy on adoption for employees adopting a child.

In order to qualify for the right to take adoption leave, you must be adopting a child through an approved adoption agency and you must have worked for the Company for a continuous period of 26 weeks calculated as at the week in which you are notified by the adoption agency of having been matched with the child for adoption.

If you are jointly adopting a child with your spouse or partner or civil partner, only one of you will be entitled to take adoption leave. You can choose which adopter will take adoption leave. The other adoptive parent will normally be entitled to take paternity leave, provided they meet the relevant eligibility criteria (see the section on Paternity Leave).

The right to adoption leave is not available to foster parents who adopt a child they are fostering, nor to step-parents who adopt their partner's child.

Notification of adoption leave

If you wish to take adoption leave, you must inform your line manager in writing of your request no later than seven days after the date on which notification of the match with the child is provided to you by the adoption agency. You must provide written details of the date on which you were notified of having been matched with the child, the date the child is expected to be placed with you for adoption and when you want your adoption leave to start. An Adoption Leave Request Form can be obtained from .... *(insert name of contact)*. As evidence of your entitlement to adoption leave, you will also be required to provide a copy of the relevant matching certificate and adoption papers from the adoption agency.

You are permitted to bring forward your adoption leave start date, provided you advise the Company in writing at least 28 days before the new start date or, if that is not possible, as soon as reasonably practicable. You may also postpone your adoption leave start date, provided you advise the Company in writing at least 28 days before the original proposed start date or, if that is not possible, as soon as reasonably practicable.

The Company will formally respond in writing to your notification of your leave plans within 28 days, confirming the date on which your adoption leave will end if you take your full 52-week entitlement to adoption leave.

Adoption leave can start on the day the child is placed with you for adoption or on a date that is up to 14 days before the expected date of placement.

Adoption leave

Assuming you are eligible, you are able to take up to a maximum of 52 weeks' adoption leave. This comprises 26 weeks' ordinary adoption leave and up to 26 weeks' additional adoption leave. This is regardless of the number of hours you work. Additional adoption leave begins on the day after ordinary adoption leave ends.

Ordinary adoption leave

During the period of ordinary adoption leave, your contract of employment continues in force and you are entitled to receive all your contractual benefits, except for salary. In particular, any benefits in kind will continue, annual leave entitlement will continue to accrue and pension contributions will continue to be made. Your pension contributions will be based on your actual pay whilst the Company's contributions will be based on the salary you would have received had you not gone on adoption leave.

Salary will be replaced by Statutory Adoption Pay (SAP) if you are eligible to receive it.

You should endeavour to take any outstanding annual leave that may be due to you before the commencement of your ordinary adoption leave. You are reminded that holiday must be taken in the year that it is earned and therefore if the holiday year is due to end during adoption leave, you should take the full year's entitlement before starting your adoption leave: see the section on Holidays for further information.

Additional adoption leave

Additional adoption leave starts immediately after the end of ordinary adoption leave and continues for a further 26 weeks.

During the period of additional adoption leave, your contract of employment continues in force and, as is the case during the period of ordinary adoption leave, you are entitled to receive all your contractual benefits, except for salary. Any benefits in kind will continue and annual leave entitlement will continue to accrue.

Salary will be replaced by SAP for the first 13 weeks of additional adoption leave if you are eligible to receive it. The remaining 13 weeks of additional adoption leave will be unpaid.

Pension contributions will continue to be made during the period when you are receiving SAP but not during any period of unpaid additional adoption leave.

Statutory Adoption Pay

SAP is payable for up to 39 weeks during adoption leave provided your average weekly earnings are not less than the lower earnings limit for National Insurance contributions. The weekly rate of SAP is paid at a rate set by the Government for the relevant tax year, or 90% of your average weekly earnings if this is lower than the Government's set weekly rate.

SAP is paid into your bank account in the same way as salary is normally paid.

SAP is treated as earnings and is therefore subject to income tax and National Insurance deductions. SAP is payable whether or not you intend to return to work after your adoption leave.

It is important for adoption pay purposes that you notify your line manager if, during the adoption pay period, you are taken into legal custody or start to work for another employer.

Contact during adoption leave

Shortly before your adoption leave starts, the Company will discuss the arrangements for you to keep in touch during your leave, should you wish to do so. The Company reserves the right in any event to maintain reasonable contact with you from time to time during your adoption leave. This may be to discuss your plans for return to work, to discuss any special arrangements to be made or training to be given to ease your return to work or simply to update you on developments at work during your absence.

Keeping in touch days

You may agree to work for the Company for up to a maximum of ten days during either your ordinary or additional adoption leave without that work bringing the period of your adoption leave to an end and without loss of a week's SAP. These are known as "keeping in touch" days. Any work carried out on a day shall constitute a day's work for these purposes.

The Company has no right to require you to carry out any work, and you have no right to undertake any work, during your adoption leave. Any work undertaken, including the amount of salary paid for any work done on keeping in touch days, is entirely a matter for agreement between the Company and you. Any keeping in touch days worked do not extend the period of your adoption leave. Once the keeping in touch days have been used up, you will lose a week's SAP for any week in which you agree to work for the Company.

Returning to work

You will have been formally advised in writing by the Company of the date on which your adoption leave will end and the date on which you are expected to return to work if you take your full 52-week entitlement to adoption leave. You are expected to return on your due return date unless you notify the Company otherwise. If you are unable to attend work at the end of your adoption leave due to sickness or injury, the Company's normal arrangements for sickness absence will apply. In any other case, late return without prior authorisation will be treated as unauthorised absence.

Whilst you are under no obligation to do so, it would assist the Company if you could confirm as soon as convenient during your adoption leave that you will be returning to work as expected.

If you wish to return to work earlier than your expected return date, you must give the Company, preferably in writing, at least eight weeks' notice of your proposed date of early return. If you fail to do so, the Company may postpone your return to such a date as will give the Company eight weeks' notice, provided that this is not later than your expected return date.

If you decide not to return to work at all after adoption leave, you must give notice of resignation in accordance with the terms of your contract of employment. If the notice period would expire after your adoption leave has ended, the Company may require you to return to work for the remainder of your notice period.

Your rights on return to work

On resuming work after ordinary adoption leave, you are entitled to return to the same job as you occupied before commencing adoption leave on the same terms and conditions as if you had not been absent. On resuming work after additional adoption leave, again you are entitled to return to the same job as you occupied before commencing adoption leave on the same terms and conditions as if you had not been absent. If, however, there is some reason why it is not reasonably practicable for the Company to take you back in your original job, you will be offered suitable alternative work of equivalent status and responsibility and on terms and conditions that are no less favourable than would have applied if you had not been absent.

Adoptions from overseas

If you adopt a child from overseas, you may still be entitled to statutory adoption leave and pay. Special rules apply in these circumstances. For further information, please contact . . . . *(insert name of contact).*

APPLICATION FORM

Please complete this application form in black ink and then return it to . . . .
(insert name of contact).

Post applied for:

Personal information		
Surname:		
Forenames:		
Title (Mr, Mrs, Miss, Ms, etc.):		
Previous names (if any):		
Current address:		
Daytime telephone number:		
Do you have the right to take up employment in the UK	YES/NO	
If you do not have the right to take up employment in the UK, would you wish us to assist you in applying for the right to work?	YES/NO	
[As at the date of submission of this application form, are you [aged over 64½] [either within six months of our Company's normal retirement age of . . . . (insert age) or over this age]?]		
Dates you are not available for interview:		
Education and qualifications From GCSE or equivalent to degree level in chronological order		
Establishment	Qualifications gained	
Postgraduate education or study or any other professional qualifications		
Establishment	Qualifications gained	

Employment history Please give details of your last three jobs, beginning with your present or most recent. Any relevant posts held before then may also be mentioned.			
From	To	Name and address of employer	Job title, description of duties and responsibilities, reason for leaving and salary on leaving.

Other information

Do you hold a full driving licence? If yes, do you have any current endorsements?

Do you have any other training, qualifications or skills relevant to the post?

Please give details of, and provide an explanation for, any time when you were not either working or in full-time education.

Have you made a previous application to the Company? If so, when was this and what was the outcome?

Please use this space to say why you are interested in the post for which you have applied and provide any other information that may assist your application.

How many weeks' or months' notice do you have to give to your current employer?

If you are disabled, please give details of any special arrangements you would require to attend interview.

Referees
Please give details of two referees, one of whom should be your current or most recent employer or, if this is an application for your first job, your school teacher or higher or further education lecturer. The other should not be a relative or contemporary.

First referee	Second referee

Declaration

I declare that the information I have given on this form is, to the best of my knowledge, true and complete. I understand that if it is subsequently discovered any statement is false or misleading, or that I have withheld relevant information, my application may be disqualified or, if I have already been appointed, I may be dismissed. I hereby give my consent to the Company processing the data supplied on this application form for the purpose of recruitment and selection.

Signed: ....

Date: ....

BONUS PAYMENT CLAUSE

The Company may, from time to time and depending on its performance and profitability and your overall performance and conduct, pay you a bonus calculated on such basis as the Company may determine. The payment or otherwise of any bonus will be wholly at the discretion of the Company. There is no contractual entitlement for you to receive a bonus at any time even if a bonus has been paid to you or to other employees on previous occasions. If a bonus is paid the amount will also be wholly at the discretion of the Company.

(The following sections can be added/deleted as appropriate.)

The period of assessment commences on . . . . . *(insert date)* each [quarter/year] and runs to . . . . *(insert date)* each [quarter/year]. The bonus is payable on . . . . *(insert date(s))*.

This discretionary bonus scheme applies to the following categories of employees only: . . . . *(insert details)*.

The payment of a bonus, and the amount of any such bonus, will depend on [you/the Company] attaining certain, specified targets.

To qualify for a bonus payment, you must still be on the payroll of the Company (and not serving notice either by resignation or dismissal) on the date the bonus is paid.

You must be employed [and have been employed by the Company for . . . . . *(insert number)* months] on the first day of the start of an assessment period to be eligible to receive a bonus for that period.

The maximum bonus payment that you may be eligible to receive will be set out in a letter to you which should be read in conjunction with these provisions. You have no entitlement to receive any minimum amount of bonus.

The Company reserves the right at any time, in its absolute discretion, to vary the maximum amount of bonus payable and/or vary the terms of the bonus scheme and/or to withdraw the bonus scheme in its entirety.

No bonus will be payable to any employee who is taking a career break on the bonus payment date. If the employee has taken a career break which spans the relevant period of assessment but has returned to work by the bonus payment date, those weeks when the employee was on a career break will be excluded in calculating the amount of any bonus payment.

In addition, under no circumstances will any bonus payment be made to any employee who has received a formal disciplinary warning under the Company's disciplinary procedure regarding their conduct or performance during the relevant period of assessment.

DISCIPLINARY PROCEDURE

Whilst the Company does not intend to impose unreasonable rules of conduct on its employees, certain standards of behaviour are necessary to maintain good employment relations and discipline in the interest of all employees. The Company prefers that discipline be voluntary and self-imposed and in the great majority of cases this is how it works. However, from time to time, it may be necessary for the Company to take action towards individuals whose level of behaviour or performance is unacceptable.

This disciplinary procedure is **entirely non-contractual** and does not form part of an employee's contract of employment.

Minor faults will be dealt with informally through counselling and training. However, in cases where informal discussion with the employee does not lead to an improvement in conduct or performance or where the matter is considered to be too serious to be classed as minor, for example, unauthorised absences, persistent poor timekeeping, sub-standard work performance, etc the following disciplinary procedure will be used. At all stages of the procedure, an investigation will be carried out.

The Company will notify the employee in writing of the allegations against him or her and will invite the employee to a disciplinary hearing to discuss the matter. The Company will provide sufficient information about the alleged misconduct or poor performance and its possible consequences to enable the employee to answer the case. This will include the provision of copies of written evidence, including witness statements, where appropriate.

Having given the employee reasonable time to prepare their case, a formal disciplinary hearing will then take place, conducted by a manager, at which the employee will be given the chance to state his or her case, accompanied if requested by a trade union official or a fellow employee of his or her choice. The employee must make every effort to attend the hearing. At the hearing, the employee will be allowed to set out their case and answer any allegations and will also be given a reasonable opportunity to ask questions, present evidence, call relevant witnesses and raise points about any information provided by witnesses.

Following the hearing, the Company will decide whether or not disciplinary action is justified and, if so, the employee will be informed in writing of the Company's decision in accordance with the stages set out below and notified of his or her right to appeal against that decision. It should be noted that an employee's behaviour is not looked at in isolation but each incident of misconduct is regarded cumulatively with any previous occurrences.

Stage 1: Written warning

The employee will be given a formal WRITTEN WARNING. He or she will be advised of the reason for the warning, how he or she needs to improve their conduct or performance, the timescale over which the improvement is to be achieved, that the warning is the first stage of the formal disciplinary procedure and the likely consequences if the terms of the warning are not complied with. The written warning will be recorded but nullified after six months, subject to satisfactory conduct and performance.

Stage 2: Final written warning

Failure to improve performance in response to the procedure so far, a repeat of misconduct for which a warning has previously been issued, or a first instance of serious misconduct or serious poor performance, will result in a FINAL WRITTEN WARNING being issued. This will set out the nature of the misconduct or poor performance, how he or she needs to improve their conduct or performance, the timescale over which the improvement is to be achieved and warn that dismissal will probably result if the terms of the warning are not complied with. This final written warning will be recorded but nullified after twelve months, subject to satisfactory conduct and performance. However, the Company reserves the right to extend the validity of the final written warning to a maximum of three years in cases of very serious misconduct or where the employee has a history of misconduct issues.

Stage 3: Dismissal

Failure to meet the requirements set out in the final written warning will normally lead to DISMISSAL with appropriate notice. A decision of this kind will only be made after the fullest possible investigation. Dismissal can be authorised only by a senior manager or a Director. The employee will be informed of the reasons for dismissal, the appropriate period of notice, the date on which his or her employment will terminate and how the employee can appeal against the dismissal decision.

Gross misconduct

Offences under this heading are so serious that an employee who commits them will normally be summarily dismissed. In such cases, the Company reserves the right to dismiss without notice of termination or payment in lieu of notice. Examples of gross misconduct include:

- any breach of the criminal law, such as theft and unauthorised possession of Company property, fraud, deliberate falsification of records or any other form of dishonesty

- wilfully causing harm or injury to another employee, physical violence, bullying or grossly offensive behaviour

- deliberately causing damage to the Company's property

- causing loss, damage or injury through serious carelessness or gross negligence

- wilful refusal to obey a reasonable management instruction or serious insubordination

- incapacity at work through an excess of alcohol or drugs

- a serious breach of health and safety rules

- harassing, bullying or victimising another employee on the grounds of race, colour, ethnic origin, nationality, national origin, religion or belief, sex, sexual orientation, gender reassignment, marital or civil partnership status, age and/or disability.

The above is intended as a guide and is not an exhaustive list.

Suspension

In the event of serious or gross misconduct, an employee may be suspended on full basic pay while a full investigation is carried out. Such suspension does not imply guilt or blame and will be for as short a period as possible. Suspension is not considered a disciplinary action.

Appeals

An employee may appeal against any disciplinary decision, including dismissal, to a Director of the Company within five working days of the decision. Appeals should be made in writing and state the grounds for appeal. The employee will be invited to attend an appeal hearing chaired by a senior manager or a Director.

At the appeal hearing, the employee will again be given the chance to state his or her case and will have the right to be accompanied by a trade union official or a fellow employee of his or her choice.

Following the appeal hearing, the employee will be informed in writing of the appeal decision. The Company's decision on an appeal will be final.

Employees who have been employed for less than one year

This disciplinary procedure does not apply to any employee who has been employed by the Company for less than one year.

EQUAL OPPORTUNITIES AND DIGNITY AT WORK POLICY

Policy statement

The Company is an equal opportunity employer and is fully committed to a policy of treating all of its employees and job applicants equally.

The Company will take all reasonable steps to employ, train and promote employees on the basis of their experience, abilities and qualifications without regard to race, colour, ethnic origin, nationality, national origin, religion or religious or philosophical belief, sex, sexual orientation, gender reassignment, age, marital or civil partnership status or disability. The Company will also take all reasonable steps to provide a work environment in which all employees are treated with respect and dignity and that is free of harassment based upon an employee's race, colour, ethnic origin, nationality, national origin, religion or religious or philosophical belief, sex, sexual orientation, gender reassignment, age, marital or civil partnership status or disability. The Company will not condone any form of harassment, whether engaged in by employees or by outside third parties who do business with the Company, such as clients, customers, contractors and suppliers.

Employees have a duty to co-operate with the Company to ensure that this policy is effective in ensuring equal opportunities and in preventing discrimination, harassment or bullying. Action will be taken under the Company's disciplinary procedure against any employee who is found to have committed an act of improper or unlawful discrimination, harassment, bullying or intimidation. Serious breaches of this equal opportunities and dignity at work statement will be treated as potential gross misconduct and could render the employee liable to summary dismissal. Employees should also bear in mind that they can be held personally liable for any act of unlawful discrimination. Employees who commit serious acts of harassment may also be guilty of a criminal offence.

You should draw the attention of your line manager to suspected discriminatory acts or practices or suspected cases of harassment. You must not victimise or retaliate against an employee who has made allegations or complaints of discrimination or harassment or who has provided information about such discrimination or harassment. Such behaviour will be treated as potential gross misconduct in accordance with the Company's disciplinary procedure.

The Company will also take appropriate action against any third parties who are found to have committed an act of improper or unlawful harassment against its employees.

Recruitment, advertising and selection

The recruitment process will be conducted in such a way as to result in the selection of the most suitable person for the job in terms of relevant experience, abilities and qualifications. The Company is committed to applying its equal opportunities policy statement at all stages of recruitment and selection.

Advertisements will encourage applications from all suitably qualified and experienced people. When advertising job vacancies, in order to attract applications from all sections of the community, the Company will, as far as reasonably practicable:

1. Ensure advertisements are not confined to those publications which would exclude or disproportionately reduce the numbers of applicants of a particular gender, sexual orientation, age, religion or racial group.

2. Avoid prescribing any unnecessary requirements which would exclude a higher proportion of a particular gender, sexual orientation, age, religion or racial group or which would exclude disabled job applicants.

3. Avoid prescribing any requirements as to marital or civil partnership status.

4. Where vacancies may be filled by promotion or transfer, they will be published to all eligible employees in such a way that they do not restrict applications from employees of any particular gender, sexual orientation, age, religion or racial group or from employees with a disability.

The selection process will be carried out consistently for all jobs at all levels. All applications will be processed in the same way. The staff responsible for short-listing, interviewing and selecting candidates will be clearly informed of the selection criteria and of the need for their consistent application. Person specifications and job descriptions will be limited to those requirements that are necessary for the effective performance of the job. Wherever possible, all applicants will be interviewed by at least two interviewers and all questions asked of the applicants will relate to the requirements of the job. The selection of new staff will be based on the job requirements and the individual's suitability and ability to do, or to train for, the job in question.

With disabled job applicants, the Company will have regard to its duty to make reasonable adjustments to work provisions, criteria and practices or to work premises in order to ensure that the disabled person is not placed at a substantial disadvantage in comparison with persons who are not disabled.

If it is necessary to assess whether personal circumstances will affect the performance of the job (for example, if the job involves unsociable hours or extensive travel), this will be discussed objectively, without detailed questions based on assumptions about race, colour, ethnic origin, nationality, national origin, religion or religious or philosophical belief, sex, sexual orientation, gender reassignment, age, marital or civil partnership status, disability, children and/or domestic obligations.

Training and promotion

The Company will train all line managers in the Company's policy on equal opportunities and in helping them identify discriminatory acts or practices or acts of harassment or bullying. Line managers will be responsible for ensuring they actively promote equal opportunity within the departments for which they are responsible.

The Company will also provide training to all employees to help them understand their rights and responsibilities in relation to dignity at work and what they can do to create a work environment that is free of bullying and harassment.

Where a promotional system is in operation, it will not be discriminatory and it will be checked from time to time to assess how it is working in practice. When a group of workers predominantly of one race, religion, sex, sexual orientation or age group or a worker with a disability appears to be excluded from access to promotion, transfer and training and to other benefits, the promotional system will be reviewed to ensure there is no unlawful discrimination.

Terms of employment, benefits, facilities and services

All terms of employment, benefits, facilities and service will be reviewed from time to time, in order to ensure that there is no unlawful discrimination on the grounds of race, colour, ethnic origin, nationality, national origin, religion or religious or philosophical belief, sex, sexual orientation, gender reassignment, age, marital or civil partnership status or disability.

Equal pay

The Company is committed to equal pay in employment. It believes its male and female employees should receive equal pay for like work, work rated as equivalent or work of equal value. In order to achieve this, the Company will endeavour to maintain a pay system that is transparent, free from bias and based on objective criteria.

Bullying and harassment

Bullying is offensive or intimidating behaviour or an abuse or misuse of power which undermines or humiliates an employee.

Harassment occurs where, on the ground of an employee's race, colour, ethnic origin, nationality, national origin, religion or religious or philosophical belief, sexual orientation, gender reassignment, age, marital or civil partnership status or disability, a person engages in unwanted conduct that:

- has the purpose of violating the employee's dignity at work, or of creating an intimidating, hostile, degrading, humiliating or offensive work environment for the employee; or

- is reasonably considered by the employee to have the effect of violating his or her dignity at work, or of creating an intimidating, hostile, degrading, humiliating or offensive work environment for the employee, even if this effect was not intended by the person responsible for the conduct.

Harassment also occurs where, related to either the employee's sex or that of another individual, a person engages in unwanted conduct that:

- has the purpose of violating the employee's dignity at work, or of creating an intimidating, hostile, degrading, humiliating or offensive work environment for the employee; or

- is reasonably considered by the employee to have the effect of violating their dignity at work, or of creating an intimidating, hostile, degrading, humiliating or offensive work environment for the employee, even if this effect was not intended by the person responsible for the conduct.

In this scenario, the employee does not need to be the subject of the unwanted conduct for harassment to have occurred - for example, the conduct could be directed at nobody in particular or at someone other than the employee, including someone of the opposite sex.

Sexual harassment (as opposed to harassment related to gender) occurs where a person engages in any form of unwanted conduct of a sexual nature that:

- has the purpose of violating the employee's dignity at work, or of creating an intimidating, hostile, degrading, humiliating or offensive work environment for the employee; or

- is reasonably considered by the employee to have the effect of violating his or her dignity at work, or of creating an intimidating, hostile, degrading, humiliating or offensive work environment for the employee, even if this effect was not intended by the person responsible for the conduct.

Conduct may be harassment whether or not the person intended to offend. Something intended as a "joke" or as "office banter" may offend another person. This is because different employees find different levels of behaviour acceptable and everyone has the right to decide for themselves what behaviour they find acceptable to them.

Behaviour which a reasonable person would realise would be likely to offend an employee will always constitute harassment without the need for the employee having to make it clear that such behaviour is unacceptable, for example, touching someone in a sexual way. With other forms of behaviour, it may not always be clear in advance that it will offend a particular employee, for example, office banter and jokes. In these cases, the behaviour will constitute harassment if the conduct continues after the employee has made it clear, by words or conduct, that such behaviour is unacceptable to him or her. A single incident can amount to harassment if it is sufficiently serious.

Harassment also occurs where, on the ground of the employee's rejection of or submission to unwanted conduct of the kind specified above, a person treats the employee less favourably than he or she would treat him or her had he or she not rejected, or submitted to, the unwanted conduct.

Examples

Bullying and harassment may be verbal, non-verbal, written or physical. Examples of unacceptable behaviour include, but are not limited to, the following:

- unwelcome sexual advances, requests for sexual favours, other conduct of a sexual nature
- subjection to obscene or other sexually suggestive or racist comments or gestures
- the offer of rewards for going along with sexual advances or threats for rejecting sexual advances
- jokes or pictures of a sexual or racial nature
- demeaning comments about an employee's appearance
- questions about a person's sex life
- the use of nick names related to an employee's sex, sexual orientation, gender reassignment, race, religion, age or disability
- picking on or ridiculing an employee
- isolating an employee or excluding him or her from social activities or relevant work-related matters.

Reporting complaints

All allegations of discrimination or harassment will be dealt with seriously, confidentially and speedily. The Company will not ignore or treat lightly grievances or complaints of discrimination or harassment from members of a particular race, colour, ethnic origin, nationality, national origin, religion or religious or philosophical belief, sex, sexual orientation or age or from employees who have undergone gender reassignment, are married, have entered into a civil partnership or have a disability.

With cases of harassment, while the Company encourages employees who believe they are being harassed to notify the offender (by words or by conduct) that his or her behaviour is unwelcome, the Company also recognises that actual or perceived power and status disparities may make such confrontation impractical.

If you wish to make a complaint of discrimination or harassment, whether against the Company, a fellow employee or a third party, you should follow the following steps:

1. First of all, report the incident of discrimination or harassment to your line manager. If you do not wish to speak to your line manager, you can instead speak to an alternative manager or to a member of the Human Resources Department.

2. Such reports should be made promptly so that investigation may proceed and any action taken expeditiously.

3. All allegations of discrimination or harassment will be taken seriously. The allegation will be promptly investigated and, as part of the investigatory process, you will be interviewed and asked to provide a written witness statement setting out the details of your complaint. Confidentiality will be maintained during the investigatory process to the extent that this is practical and appropriate in the circumstances. However, in order to effectively investigate an allegation, the Company must be able to determine the scope of the investigation and the individuals who should be informed of or interviewed about the allegation. For example, the identity of the complainant and the nature of the allegations must be revealed to the alleged harasser or discriminator so that he or she is able to fairly respond to the allegations. The Company reserves the right to arrange for another manager to conduct the investigation other than the manager with whom you raised the matter.

4. Once the investigation has been completed, you will be informed in writing of the outcome and the Company's conclusions and decision as soon as possible. The Company is committed to taking appropriate action with respect to all complaints of discrimination or harassment which are upheld.

5. You will not be penalised for raising a complaint, even if it is not upheld, unless your complaint was both untrue and made in bad faith.

6. If your complaint is upheld and the harasser or discriminator remains in the Company's employment, the Company will take all reasonable steps to ensure that you do not have to continue working alongside him or her if you do not wish to do so. The Company will discuss the options with you.

7. If your complaint is not upheld, arrangements will be made for you and the alleged harasser or discriminator to continue or resume working and to repair working relationships.

Alternatively, you may, if you wish, use the Company's grievance procedure to make a complaint.

Any employee who is found to have discriminated against or harassed another employee in violation of this policy will be subject to disciplinary action under the Company's disciplinary procedure. Such behaviour may be treated as gross misconduct and could render the employee liable to summary dismissal. In addition, line managers who had knowledge that such discrimination or harassment had occurred in their departments but who had taken no action to eliminate it will also be subject to disciplinary action under the Company's disciplinary procedure.

Monitoring equal opportunity and dignity at work

The Company will regularly monitor the effects of selection decisions and personnel and pay practices and procedures in order to assess whether equal opportunity and dignity at work are being achieved. This will also involve considering any possible indirectly discriminatory effects of its working practices. If changes are required, the Company will implement them. The Company will also make reasonable adjustments to its standard working practices to overcome barriers caused by disability.

FLEXIBILITY CLAUSE

Your core working hours are from .... *(insert time)* to .... *(insert time)*. However, in order to meet the needs of the business, you may be required to work additional hours as are reasonably necessary in order to carry out your duties effectively. Please note that, unless specifically agreed with your line manager, such time will be unpaid.

FLEXIBLE JOB DUTIES CLAUSE

There will be times when you may be required to undertake additional tasks, duties and responsibilities within your capabilities. The Company reserves the right to vary your tasks, duties and responsibilities at any time and from time to time according to the needs of the Company's business. However, you will not be assigned to duties or required to perform services which you cannot reasonably perform or which are outside the range of your normal skills and experience. There will also be times when you may be asked to transfer, either temporarily or permanently, to an alternative job within the Company. Where this is agreed with you, either on a temporary or a permanent basis, it will be confirmed to you in writing.

FLEXIBLE WORKING ACCEPTANCE LETTER

Date .... *(insert date)*

Dear .... *(insert name of employee)*

Following receipt of your flexible working application and our meeting on ....
(insert date), I have considered your request for a new flexible working pattern.

I am pleased to confirm that the Company is able to accommodate your application.

OR

Unfortunately, as explained to you at the meeting, the Company is unable to accommodate your original request. However, as we also discussed, I am able to offer you an alternative working pattern, which you agreed would be suitable to you.

Your new working pattern will be as follows: ....
(insert details of the new day/hours/times of work).

Your new working arrangements will begin from .... *(insert date)*.

Please note that the change in your working pattern represents a permanent change to your terms and conditions of employment and you have no right in law to revert back to your previous working pattern.

If you have any questions on the information provided in this letter, please contact ..
.... *(insert name of contact)* to discuss them as soon as possible.
Please sign the attached duplicate copy of this letter and return it to ....
(insert name of contact) to signify your agreement to the changes set out above.

Yours sincerely

....

(Insert signature and name of author)

Enc

I accept the permanent change to my terms and conditions of employment set out in this flexible working acceptance letter dated .... *(insert date)*.

Signed: ....

Date: ....

FLEXIBLE WORKING POLICY

It is the Company's view that the promotion of flexible working arrangements increases staff motivation, performance and productivity, reduces stress and encourages staff retention by enabling employees to balance their work life with their other priorities.

The statutory right

Employees who are parents of children aged under 17 or disabled children aged under 18 have a statutory right to apply for a change to the terms and conditions of their employment to have flexible working arrangements to look after their children. Employees who are carers of specified categories of adults have the same statutory right. In order to make a request under the statutory right, you must have worked for the Company for a continuous period of six months at the date of application. You must also meet *each* of the following eligibility criteria:

Childcare

- you have responsibility for the upbringing of either a child under 17 or a disabled child under 18

- you are either the mother, father, adopter, guardian, special guardian, foster parent or private foster carer of the child, or you have a residence order relating to the child, or you are married to or the partner or civil partner of the child's mother, father, adopter, guardian, special guardian, foster parent or private foster carer or a person in whose favour a residence order is in force in respect of the child.

- you are making the request to help care for the child

- you are making the request no later than the day before the child's 17th birthday or 18th birthday where the child is disabled.

- you have worked continuously for the Company for the previous 26 weeks

- you have not made a request to work flexibly under the statutory right during the past twelve months.

Adult care

- you are making this request to help care for an adult aged 18 or over who is either married to you, or is your partner or civil partner, or is your relative or who lives at the same address as you. For these purposes a "relative" means a mother, father, adopter, guardian, special guardian, parent-in-law, step-parent, son, son-in-law, step-son, daughter, daughter-in-law, step-daughter, brother, step-brother, brother-in-law, sister, step-sister, sister-in-law, uncle, aunt or grandparent, and this includes adoptive relationships and relationships of the full blood or half blood or, in the case of an adopted person, such of those relationships as would exist but for the adoption

- you have worked continuously for the Company for the previous 26 weeks

- you have not made a request to work flexibly under the statutory right during the past twelve months.

Flexible working generally

In addition to statutory rights, it is the Company's policy to try and be flexible on working patterns for all employees, although priority will always be given to those employees who do have the statutory right to request flexible working so that the Company can comply with its legal obligations. You may therefore wish to apply for flexible working to accommodate charity work, leisure activities, other caring arrangements or external study. All employees are eligible to apply for flexible working regardless of their seniority, current working pattern, age, sex, race, religion, sexual orientation, whether they have a disability or whether they are employed on a permanent or fixed-term basis.

You can apply to vary the number of hours you work, the times you work or your place of work (between your home and the Company's place of business).Although the Company is committed to being flexible on working patterns for its employees, you must recognise that the requirements of the business are paramount and it may not be appropriate or possible for flexible working arrangements to apply to all jobs across all areas of the business.

The flexible working application procedure

You should comply with the following procedure to make your application for flexible working arrangements:

- make your request in writing setting out the flexible working arrangement you seek. A Flexible Working Application Form can be obtained from . . . .
  (insert name of contact)

- within 28 days of receipt of your application, the Company will set up a meeting with you to discuss the changes you have proposed, the effect of the proposed changes and any possible alternative work patterns that might suit. You may be accompanied at this meeting by a work colleague

- the Company will consider your request and will make a practical business assessment on whether, and if so, how it could be accommodated

- the Company will notify its decision to you within 14 days of the meeting. If the Company accepts your request, it will write to you, establishing a start date and providing a written note of the contract of employment variation. If your application is refused, the Company will explain the grounds for refusal in writing and confirm the internal appeal procedure

- where your request is agreed to, it constitutes a permanent change to your terms and conditions of employment. This means you do not have the right to revert to your previous pattern of working at a future date

- you can appeal in writing against a refusal within 14 days of receipt of the Company's rejection letter. The Company will then set up a meeting with you to discuss your appeal within 14 days after receiving your appeal letter. After that meeting has been held, the Company will write to you within 14 days to notify you of the outcome of your appeal.

Grounds for refusal

The Company may refuse your flexible working application on one or more of the following grounds:

- the burden of additional costs

- the detrimental effect it would have on the Company's ability to meet customer demand

- the Company's inability to reorganise work amongst existing staff

- the Company's inability to recruit additional staff

- the detrimental impact it would have on quality

- the detrimental impact it would have on performance

- the insufficiency of work available during the period when you propose to work

- the Company's planned structural changes.

In refusing an application, the Company will provide details relating to why the particular ground applies in the circumstances.

Please note that each request for flexible working will be dealt with individually, taking into account the likely effects the changes will have on the Company, the work of the department in which you are employed, your work colleagues and the particular circumstances of the case. This means that if the Company agrees to one employee's request, this does not set a precedent or create a right for another employee to be granted the same or a similar change to their work pattern.

FLEXIBLE WORKING REJECTION LETTER

Date . . . . *(insert date)*

Dear . . . . *(insert name of employee)*

Following receipt of your flexible working application and our meeting on . . . . *(insert date)*, I have considered your request for a new, flexible working pattern.

Unfortunately, having given full consideration to your application, I regret that the Company is unable to accommodate your request. The reasons for this are set out below.

You requested a reduction to your working hours/a change to the pattern of your working hours/a change to your place of work*. It is the Company's view that agreeing to these changes would:

- impose an unreasonable burden of additional costs on the Company*

- have a detrimental effect on the Company's ability to meet its customers' demands*

- have a detrimental impact on quality*

- have a detrimental impact on performance*

- create unacceptable difficulties for the Company as we have been unable to make arrangements to reorganise the work amongst the other staff*

- create unacceptable difficulties for the Company as we have been/would be unable to recruit additional staff*

- create unacceptable difficulties for the Company due to an insufficiency of work during the periods you proposed to work*

- be inappropriate due to structural changes the Company is planning.*

(*Delete as appropriate.)

The business grounds listed above apply to your request for a new flexible working pattern because . . . . *(explain in more detail why the business grounds apply in the circumstances. An explanation of around two paragraphs will usually suffice).*

In addition, the other alternative work patterns we discussed at the meeting are inappropriate for the same reasons set out above.

If you are unhappy with the Company's decision to refuse your request for flexible working you have the right to appeal against it. If you wish to appeal, you must write to . . . . *(insert name of contact)*, setting out the grounds for your appeal, within 14 days of receipt of this letter. . . . . *(insert name of contact)* will then arrange a meeting with you to discuss your appeal within 14 days after receiving your appeal letter. After that meeting has been held, ... *(insert name of contact)* will then write to you within 14 days to notify you of the outcome of your appeal.

Yours sincerely

. . . .

(Insert signature and name of author)

GRIEVANCE PROCEDURE

Policy

The primary purpose of this grievance procedure is to enable staff to air any concerns that they may have about practices, policies or treatment from other individuals at work or from the Company, and to produce a speedy resolution where genuine problems exist. It is designed to help all employees to take the appropriate action, when they are experiencing difficulties, in an atmosphere of trust and collaboration.

Although it may not be possible to solve all problems to everyone's complete satisfaction, this policy forms an undertaking by the Company that it will deal objectively and constructively with all employee grievances, and that anyone who decides to use the procedure may do so with the confidence that their problem will be dealt with fairly.

This grievance procedure is not a substitute for good day-to-day communication in the Company where we encourage employees to discuss and resolve daily working issues in a supportive atmosphere. Many problems can be solved on an informal footing very satisfactorily if all employees are prepared to keep the channels of communication between themselves open and working well. This procedure is designed to deal with those issues that need to be approached on a more formal basis so that every route to a satisfactory solution can be explored and so that any decisions reached are binding and long lasting.

This grievance procedure is **entirely non-contractual** and does not form part of an employee's contract of employment.

Procedure

If you cannot settle your grievance informally, you should raise it formally. This procedure has been drawn up to establish the appropriate steps to be followed when pursuing and dealing with a formal grievance.

Stage 1

In the event of your having a formal grievance relating to your employment you should, in the first instance, put your grievance in writing and address it to your line manager, making clear that you wish to raise a formal grievance under the terms of this procedure. Where your grievance is against your line manager, your complaint should be addressed to an alternative manager or to the human resources department. This grievance procedure will not be invoked unless you raise your grievance in accordance with these requirements.

A manager (who may not be the manager to whom your grievance was addressed) will then invite you to attend a grievance meeting to discuss your grievance and you have the right to be accompanied at this meeting by a trade union official or a fellow employee of your choice. Every effort will be made to convene the grievance meeting at a time which is convenient for you and your companion to attend. If this means that the meeting cannot be held within a reasonable period (usually within five working days of the original date set), we ask that you make arrangements with another companion who is available to attend. Any employee who is chosen to accompany another in a grievance hearing is entitled to take paid time off for this purpose.

You must make every effort to attend the grievance meeting.

At the meeting, you will be permitted to explain your grievance and how you think it should be resolved.

Following the meeting, the Company will endeavour to respond to your grievance as soon as possible and, in any case, within five working days of the grievance meeting. If it is not possible to respond within this time period, you will be given an explanation for the delay and be told when a response can be expected. You will be informed in writing of the Company's decision on the grievance and notified of your right to appeal against that decision if you are not satisfied with it.

Stage 2

In the event that you feel your grievance has not been satisfactorily resolved, you may then appeal in writing to a Director of the Company within five working days of the grievance decision. You should also set out the grounds for your appeal.

On receipt of your appeal letter, a more senior manager or a Director (who again may not be the person to whom your appeal was addressed) shall make arrangements to hear your grievance at an appeal meeting and at this meeting you may again, if you wish, be accompanied by a trade union official or a fellow employee of your choice.

You must make every effort to attend the grievance appeal meeting.

Following the meeting, the senior manager or Director will endeavour to respond to your grievance as soon as possible and, in any case, within five working days of the appeal hearing. If it is not possible to respond within this time period, you will be given an explanation for the delay and be told when a response can be expected. You will be informed in writing of the Company's decision on your grievance appeal.

This is the final stage of the grievance procedure and the Company's decision shall be final.

Disciplinary issues

If your complaint relates to your dissatisfaction with a disciplinary, performance review or dismissal decision, you should not invoke the grievance procedure but should instead appeal against that decision in accordance with the appeal procedure with which you will have been provided.

HEALTH AND SAFETY POLICY

The Company is committed to ensuring the health, safety and welfare of its employees, and it will, so far as is reasonably practicable, establish procedures and systems necessary to implement this commitment and to comply with its statutory obligations on health and safety. It is the responsibility of each employee to familiarise themselves and comply with the Company's procedures and systems on health and safety.

While the Company will take all reasonable steps to ensure the health and safety of its employees, health and safety at work is also the responsibility of the employees themselves. It is the duty of each employee to take reasonable care of their own and other people's health, safety and welfare and to report any situation which may pose a serious or imminent threat to the well being of themselves or of any other person. If an employee is unsure how to perform a certain task or feels it would be dangerous to perform a specific job or use specific equipment, then it is the employee's duty to report this as soon as possible to their line manager, their health and safety representative or the safety officer. Alternatively, an employee may, if they prefer, invoke the Company's formal grievance procedure or they may make a complaint under the Company's provisions on Disclosures in the Public Interest.

Disciplinary action under the Company's disciplinary procedure may be taken against any employee who violates health and safety rules and procedures or who fails to perform their duties under health and safety legislation. Depending on the seriousness of the offence, it may amount to potential gross misconduct rendering the employee liable to summary dismissal.

The Company will provide and maintain a healthy and safe working environment with the objective of minimising the number of instances of occupational accidents and illnesses.

The Company will pay particular attention to:

1. Maintaining the workplace in a safe condition and providing adequate facilities and arrangements for welfare at work.

2. Providing a safe means of access to and egress from the workplace.

3. The provision and maintenance of equipment and systems of work that are safe.

4. Arrangements for ensuring safety to health in connection with the use, handling, storage and transport of articles and substances.

5. The provision of such information, instructions, training and supervision as is necessary to ensure the health and safety at work of its employees and other persons.

The Company also recognises its duty to protect the health and safety of all visitors to the Company, including contractors and temporary workers, as well as any members of the public who might be affected by the Company's work operations.

Organisation

The Board of the Company has overall responsibility for health and safety in the Company . . . . (insert name of contact) is the safety officer and has responsibility for overseeing, implementing and monitoring health and safety procedures in the Company and for reporting back to the Board on health and safety matters. The safety officer also conducts regular inspections of the workplace, maintains safety records and investigates and reports on accidents at work.

In addition, a number of employees have been delegated as health and safety representatives. Further details can be obtained from . . . . . (insert name of contact).

Training

Safety training is an integral part of an effective health and safety programme. It is essential that every employee is trained to perform their job safely. All employees will be trained in safe working practices and procedures. Training will include instruction on the safe use of any equipment provided.

Employees at special risk

The Company recognises that some workers may from time to time be at increased risk of injury or ill-health resulting from work activities. The Company therefore requires that all employees advise their line manager if they become aware of any change in their personal circumstances which could result in their being at increased risk. This could include medical conditions, permanent or temporary disability, taking medication and pregnancy.

First aid and reporting accidents at work

First aid boxes are located at strategic points around the workplace. All employees will be shown the location of the nearest first aid box and will be given the names of the designated first aid personnel. This information is also displayed on works notice boards.

All injuries, however small, sustained by a person at work must be reported to their line manager or the safety officer and recorded in the accident book. Accident records are crucial to the effective monitoring of health and safety procedures and must therefore be accurate and comprehensive. The safety officer will inspect the accident book on a regular basis and all accidents will be investigated and a report prepared, with any necessary action being taken to prevent a recurrence of the problem.

Fire

Fire is a significant risk within the workplace. All employees have a duty to conduct their operations in such a way as to minimise the risk of fire and they are under a duty to report immediately any fire, smoke or potential fire hazards, such as faulty electric cable or loose connections. Employees should never attempt to repair or interfere with electrical equipment or wiring themselves. The safety officer is responsible for the maintenance and testing of fire alarms and fire fighting, prevention and detection equipment.

Smoke detectors and manually operated fire alarms are located at strategic points throughout the workplace. If a smoke detector sounds or fire is discovered, it is the responsibility of any employee present to activate the alarm and evacuate the building. Fire extinguishers are also located at strategic points throughout the workplace. Employees are expected to tackle a fire themselves only if it would pose no threat to their personal safety to do so. If the situation is dangerous or potentially dangerous, the employee should activate the fire alarm and evacuate the building immediately.

Fire doors designed to slow the spread of fire and smoke throughout the workplace have been installed at strategic points. Fire doors are designed to close automatically after opening and must never be blocked or wedged open. Fire exits are also located at strategic points throughout the workplace. Fire exit doors and corridors must never be locked, blocked or used as storage space. All employees must ensure they are familiar with their evacuation route and designated assembly point in case of fire. Practice fire drills will be conducted on a regular basis to ensure employee familiarity with emergency evacuation procedures.

Emergency lighting has been installed in exit corridors and above emergency exit doors in case of power failure. Lifts also have emergency lighting installed although they should not be used in the case of an emergency evacuation.

Company safety rules

- all employees should be aware of and adhere to the Company's rules and procedures on health and safety

- all employees must immediately report any unsafe working practices or conditions to their line manager, their health and safety representative or to the safety officer

- horseplay, practical joking, running in the workplace, misuse of equipment or any other acts which might jeopardise the health and safety of any other person are forbidden

- any person whose levels of alertness are reduced due to illness or fatigue will not be allowed to work if this might jeopardise the health and safety of any person

- employees must not adjust, move or otherwise tamper with any electrical equipment or machinery in a manner not within the scope of their job duties

- all waste materials must be disposed of carefully in the receptacles provided and in such a way that they do not constitute a hazard to other workers

- no employee should undertake a job which appears to be unsafe

- no employee should undertake a job until they have received adequate safety instruction and they are authorised to carry out the task

- all injuries must be reported to the employee's line manager or to the safety officer

- all materials must be properly and safely used and when not in use properly and safely secured

- work should be well-planned to avoid injuries in the handling of heavy materials and while using equipment

- employees should take care to ensure that all protective guards and other safety devices are properly fitted and in good working order and must immediately report any defects to their line manager or to the safety officer

- suitable clothing and footwear must be worn at all times. Personal protective equipment must be worn where appropriate

- work stations and work sites must be kept clean and tidy and any spillage must be cleaned up immediately

- employees should use handrails when going up and down stairs, should never read while walking, must close filing cabinet drawers when not in use and must keep all floor areas free of obstruction.

Access

- walkways and passageways must be kept clear and free from obstructions at all times

- if a walkway or passageway becomes wet it should be clearly marked with warning signs and any liquid spilt on the floor should be wiped up immediately

- trailing cables should not be left in any passageway

- where objects are stored in or around a passageway, care must be taken to ensure that no long or sharp edges jut out into the passageway

- where a passageway is being used by vehicles or other moving machinery, an alternative route should be used by pedestrians where possible. If no alternative route is available, the area must be clearly marked with warning signs.

Tools and equipment

- Company machinery, tools and equipment are only to be used by qualified and authorised personnel

- it is the responsibility of all employees to ensure that any tools or equipment they use are in a good and safe condition. Any tools or equipment which are defective must be reported to a line manager or to the safety officer

- all tools must be properly and safely stored when not in use

- no tool should be used without the manufacturer's recommended shields, guards or attachments

- approved personal protective equipment must be properly used where appropriate

- persons using machine tools must not wear clothing, jewellery or long hair in such a way as might pose a risk to their own or anyone else's safety

- employees are prohibited from using any tool or piece of equipment for any purpose other than its intended purpose.

Manual handling

- lifting and moving of objects should always be done by mechanical devices rather than manual handling wherever reasonably practicable. The equipment used should be appropriate for the task at hand

- the load to be lifted or moved must be inspected for sharp edges and wet patches

- when lifting or moving a load with sharp or splintered edges, gloves must be worn

- the route over which the load is to be lifted should be inspected to ensure it is free of obstructions

- employees should not attempt to lift or move a load which is too heavy to manage comfortably. Employees should ask for assistance if there is any danger of strain

- when lifting an object off the ground, employees should assume a squatting position, keeping the back straight. The load should be lifted by straightening the knees, not the back

- employees should not attempt to obtain items from shelves which are beyond their reach. A ladder or stepping stool should be used. Employees should not use chairs or any makeshift device for climbing and should never climb up the shelves themselves.

HOLIDAY PAY ON TERMINATION CLAUSE

On termination of your employment, you will be paid in lieu for holiday accrued but not taken in that holiday year only. Unless required by law, on termination of your employment, you have no right to be paid for holiday accrued but not taken in previous holiday years.

If, on termination, you have taken more holiday than you have earned in that holiday year, the Company shall be entitled as a result of your agreement to the terms of this contract to deduct the value of the unearned holiday from any final payment of salary made to you.

HOLIDAYS POLICY

Your paid annual leave entitlement is set out in your Statement of Terms and Conditions of Employment.

The Company's holiday year runs from . . . .*(insert date)* to . . . . *(insert date)*. You must use all of your holiday entitlement by the last day of each holiday year and, unless there are exceptional circumstances and unless approved in writing in advance by your line manager, you may not carry your holiday entitlement forward into the next holiday year. Holiday entitlement not used by the correct date will usually be lost and under no circumstances will payment in lieu be made for holiday entitlement that is lost through not being exercised by the correct date.

Your line manager must approve all requests for annual leave in writing in advance. You must not book holidays until your request has been formally authorised. You should endeavour to give as much notice as possible of proposed annual leave dates. In any event, such notice must be at least twice the number of days' leave as that you wish to take as annual leave. The Company will try to co-operate with your holiday plans where possible, but this is always subject to the requirements of the Company's business and to adequate staffing levels being maintained at all times.

. . . . *(insert number)* days of your annual holiday entitlement must be taken, e.g. during the off-peak summer months/at Christmas, when the Company operates a shutdown. The Company will give you notice of the exact dates you are required to take as annual leave as early as possible after the start of the holiday year and in any event at least one month in advance of the shutdown.

No more than two weeks' paid annual leave may be taken at any one time without the prior written agreement of your line manager.

In your first and last year of employment, your holiday entitlement will be that proportion of your annual holiday entitlement equivalent to the proportion of the holiday year in question during which you have been employed. This will be calculated to the nearest half day and assuming that holiday entitlement accrues at an even rate from day to day. During your first year of service, unless otherwise agreed in writing by your line manager, you will not normally be permitted to take more annual leave than you have actually accrued at the time the holiday is taken. Entitlement during your first year of service is calculated monthly in advance at the rate of one-twelfth of the full year's entitlement.

Should you be incapacitated for work due to sickness or injury during any period of pre-booked annual leave (whether in whole or in part) the Company may in its absolute discretion reimburse the period of annual leave entitlement lost due to incapacity. You have no contractual right to reimbursement and, before considering whether reimbursement is appropriate in the circumstances, you must deliver to the Company a relevant medical certificate covering the period of incapacity. Reimbursement will only be considered where you fell seriously ill or you sustained a serious injury.

Only statutory annual leave entitlement provided for in the **Working Time Regulations 1998** will accrue during a period of long-term sickness absence. Any additional contractual annual leave provided for in your Statement of Terms and Conditions of Employment that is over and above the statutory minimum annual leave entitlement will not accrue during a period of long-term sickness absence, except at the absolute discretion of the Company.

If you are absent due to long-term incapacity, you are encouraged to apply to take your accrued holiday entitlement before the end of the holiday year. However, in exceptional cases of long-term incapacity and if approved in writing by your line manager, you may be permitted to carry forward some or all of your accrued holiday entitlement into the next holiday year if either you are still off sick at the end of the holiday year or there is insufficient time remaining on your return to work in the holiday year to take your full accrued entitlement. The Company may also, at its absolute discretion, request you to take your accrued annual holiday entitlement during a period of long-term sickness absence before the end of the holiday year and the Company will not be obliged to give you any minimum period of notice to request you to take your annual leave in this case. However, if you do not wish to take annual leave during your sickness absence, you may notify the Company in writing that you decline this request, provided that you do so before the period of annual leave commences. At the end of the period of annual leave if you do take it, you will revert back to long-term sickness absence unless you are medically fit to return to work.

During your notice period (whether notice of termination of employment is given by the Company or by you), the Company may require you to take any outstanding accrued annual leave that you may have and the Company will not be obliged to give you any minimum notice to take such annual leave during your notice period.

On the termination of your employment, you are entitled to be paid in lieu for any accrued annual leave for that holiday year that has not been taken by the date of termination. Unless required by law, on the termination of your employment, you have no right to be paid for holiday accrued but not taken in previous holiday years.

If, on the date of termination of your employment, you have taken more annual leave than you have accrued in that holiday year, you will be required to reimburse the Company in respect of such unearned annual leave. The Company shall be entitled to deduct the value of the unearned annual leave from any final payment of salary to be made to you. Holiday pay will be at a rate derived from annual salary accruing at . . . . *(insert number)* days per month.

No payment in lieu of accrued contractual annual leave will be made to you in the event of the termination of your employment for gross misconduct or in the event that you give inadequate notice to terminate your employment or you leave before your contractual notice period has expired. For these purposes, contractual annual leave means any leave entitlement provided for in your contract of employment that is over and above the statutory annual leave entitlement provided for in the **Working Time Regulations 1998**.

JOB DESCRIPTION

Job title *(insert the name by which the job is usually known)*:

....

Department *(insert the section of the Company where the post holder will be working)*:

....

Responsible to *(insert the job title of the line manager of this post)*:

....

Responsible for *(insert the job titles of any staff to be supervised by the post holder)*:

....

Job purpose *(insert a brief description of the role that this position covers)*:

....

Main duties *(insert a list of the main job duties. List and number them in order of importance)*:

....

....

....

Additional duties *(insert a list of other duties that the post holder may be required to undertake from time to time)*:

....

....

....

Main responsibilities *(insert a list of the post holder's responsibilities, including any delegated authority they may have)*:

....

....

....

Prepared by *(insert the name and job title of the person who prepared the job description)*:

....

....

Date *(insert the date for future reference)*:

....

The Company reserves the right to vary or amend the duties and responsibilities of the post holder at any time according to the needs of the Company's business.

PERSON SPECIFICATION

Qualities	Essential	Desirable

Educational attainments

General education equivalent to

Knowledge and experience

Knowledge of

Understanding of

Experience in

General intelligence

Tests

General reasoning ability

Skills and special aptitudes

Mechanical

Manual dexterity

Skill with words

Skill with numbers

Ability to

Artistic ability

Musical ability

Interests

Intellectual

Practical/constructional

Physically active

Community

Qualities	Essential	Desirable

Disposition and personal qualities

Reliability

Stability

Discretion and diplomacy

Leadership

Impartiality of judgment

Self-reliance and self-motivation

Circumstances

Mobility

Domicile

Date: ....

Prepared by: ....

LAY-OFF AND SHORT TIME WORKING CLAUSE

The Company reserves the right to lay you off or put you on short time working where the needs of the Company's business make this necessary, for example because there is a temporary cessation of or reduction in work or a temporary closure of the workplace. You will be notified of the lay-off or short time working, the date when it will start and how long it is anticipated to last for. The position will then be kept under regular review by the Company.

In the event that you are laid off or put on short time working, your entitlement to pay on workless days in that period of lay-off or short time working will cease and instead, if you qualify, you will be paid guarantee payments at the prevailing statutory rate during that period. Guarantee payments are paid for a maximum of the first five workless days within a three-month period.

Your continuity of employment will not be affected by a lay-off or short time working.

LEAVES OF ABSENCE POLICY

Paid annual leave

The provisions relating to your entitlement to paid annual leave are set out in your contract of employment and in the section on Holidays.

Religious holidays

Subject to complying with the relevant provisions as to the notice set out in your contract of employment and to the requirements of the Company's business, you will normally be allowed to use your annual leave entitlement to observe special religious holidays.

Jury service and witness attendance

Should you be called up for jury service or required to attend court to give evidence as a witness, you must notify your line manager as soon as reasonably practicable. Time off work will normally be granted in these circumstances. You will be required to provide a copy of the court summons to support your request for time off work.

You have no contractual or statutory right to be paid for time not worked due to jury service or witness attendance. Any payment of salary by the Company during this period is done so in its absolute discretion and will be subject to the deduction of any monies received from the court in respect of loss of earnings. You must therefore submit a claim to the court for loss of earnings and claim the full allowance available to you.

If on any day on which you attend court you are told that your services are not required, you must then return to work and report to your line manager before starting work.

Other public duties

If you are a justice of the peace, you have a statutory right to take a reasonable amount of unpaid time off work for the purpose of performing any of the duties of the office.

If you are a member of one of the following bodies, you also have a statutory right to take a reasonable amount of unpaid time off work for the purpose of attendance at meetings of the body, or any of its committees, or undertaking other duties approved by the body for the purpose of discharging the body's functions:

- a local authority

- a statutory tribunal

- a police authority

- an independent monitoring board for a prison or a prison visiting committee

- a relevant health body (e.g. an NHS trust, an NHS foundation trust, a Strategic Health Authority, a Special Health Authority or a Primary Care Trust)

- a relevant education body (e.g. a managing or governing body of an educational establishment maintained by a local education authority, a governing body of a further or higher education corporation or the General Teaching Council for England or Wales)

- the Environment Agency or the Scottish Environment Protection Agency, or

- Scottish Water or a Water Customer Consultation Panel.

You have no contractual or statutory right to be paid for time not worked due to performing public duties. Any payment of salary by the Company during this period is done so in its absolute discretion.

Membership of the reserved armed forces

If you are a member of the reserved armed forces, you may use your paid annual leave entitlement to carry out your duties, provided you comply with the provisions relating to paid annual leave set out in your contract of employment and in the section on "Holidays". The Company expects you to use your paid annual leave first before applying for further time off.

Otherwise, any further time off relating to membership of the reserved armed forces will only be granted at the absolute discretion of the Company and you have no contractual or statutory right to be paid for this leave. Any payment of salary made by the Company in such circumstances is done so in its absolute discretion.

If you wish to apply for this type of leave, you should apply in writing to . . . . *(insert name of contact)* stating the period of leave requested and the reasons for it.

Medical appointments

Appointments with doctors, dentists and other medical practitioners should, as far as reasonably practicable, be made outside of your normal hours of work or with the minimum disruption to the working day (i.e. made at the beginning or end of the working day).

Time off work to attend medical appointments must be authorised by your line manager in advance. In any event, unless there are exceptional circumstances, no more than two hours should be taken off work for any one appointment. You have no contractual or statutory right to be paid for absences relating to attendance at medical appointments. Any payment of salary during attendance at such appointments is made at the absolute discretion of the Company.

Compassionate leave

Subject to your statutory right to time off to deal with a family emergency (see the section on Time Off for Dependants), if you suffer a bereavement or serious illness in your family or in a close relationship, compassionate leave must be approved by your line manager. All requests for compassionate leave will be considered on an individual basis.

There is no contractual or statutory entitlement to be paid for absences relating to compassionate leave. Any payment of salary during compassionate leave is made at the absolute discretion of the Company.

Subject to your statutory right to time off to deal with a family emergency, the Company expects you to use your paid annual leave entitlement for time off needed to care for sick relatives or friends.

Special unpaid leave

The Company may, in certain circumstances, consider requests for special unpaid leave, for example, for the purposes of education, family responsibilities or for important personal reasons. However, the Company expects you to use your paid annual leave first. Otherwise, any further time off for special reasons will only be granted at the absolute discretion of the Company and you have no contractual or statutory right to be paid for this leave. If you wish to apply for special leave, you should do so in writing to . . . . *(insert name of contact)* stating the period of leave requested and the reasons for it. Requests for special leave will be assessed on their individual merits and circumstances. Special leave is operated entirely at the discretion of the Company and it may be withdrawn at any time.

[Career breaks and sabbaticals

The Company may, at its absolute discretion and subject to certain conditions being satisfied, permit employees to take a career break or sabbatical and then return to work at the end of that break. The conditions that must be satisfied are:

- a career break must be for an agreed duration which is between [for example one month] and [for example, one year]

- career breaks will only be available to employees who have a minimum of [for example, three] years' continuous employment with the Company

- employees must make a request for a career break at least [for example, two months] before the proposed start date

- the purpose of the career break must be agreed with the Company in advance and a career break will not be granted where the intended purpose is to enable the employee to take up other paid employment. A career break can be used for a variety of purposes, such as time off to undergo a college or university course, on account of family responsibilities, to allow an employee to pursue a personal interest or undertake voluntary work, for overseas travel or for any other purpose agreed with the Company.

Any career break granted will be unpaid.

If you are granted a career break, your continuity of employment will be broken by that break and your contract of employment will terminate on your last day of work immediately before your career break commences. When you therefore return to work at the end of the career break, this will be a new period of employment with the Company and neither the period of your previous employment with the Company prior to the career break nor the career break itself will count as part of your continuous period of employment with the Company. You should also be aware that the loss of continuity of employment will have an impact on any statutory rights or contractual benefits that are linked to or dependent on continued employment or length of service.

If you would like to be considered for a career break, you should apply in writing to . . . . (insert name of contact) stating the purpose for which you wish to take the break, when you would like it to start, the intended length of the break and the date on which you would propose to return to work. You have no contractual right to take a career break and any request you may make will be considered in line with the operational needs of the Company's business.

If the Company agrees to grant you a career break, this will be on the basis that you agree to return to work on a specified date. Providing this and the other conditions for career breaks are met, you will be able to return to work with the Company at the end of the career break. This will be a return to the same job on the same terms and conditions as you occupied before the career break, unless a redundancy situation has arisen. If, however, there is some reason other than redundancy why it is not reasonably practicable for you to be taken back in your original job, you will be offered alternative work on terms and conditions which are no less favourable overall than the terms and conditions of employment which applied to you immediately before your career break. On your return to work, the Company may, at its absolute discretion, require you to undertake a period of retraining as necessary.

Except where you are ill and you have followed the Company's normal procedures in relation to sickness absence, if you fail to return to work on the agreed return date at the end of a career break, you will forfeit your right to return to work with the Company. You will then not be able to return to work at a later date.]

[Elective surgery

Elective surgery is surgery that is not considered to be medically necessary, for example because it is concerned with the enhancement of appearance through surgical and medical techniques. It includes cosmetic surgery (such as breast implants and face-lifts) and other non-essential medical procedures such as laser eye treatment and vasectomies.

[If you wish to take time off for elective surgery, you may use your existing paid annual leave entitlement, provided you comply with the provisions relating to annual leave set out in your contract of employment and in the section on "Holidays".]

[At its absolute discretion, the Company may grant you up to . . . . . (*insert number*) days' leave in any one calendar year to undergo elective surgery. Elective surgery must be arranged at a time that will cause the minimum amount of inconvenience to the Company. If you require further time off, you may use your existing paid annual leave entitlement, provided you comply with the provisions relating to annual leave set out in your contract of employment and in the section on "Holidays".]

[You have no contractual or statutory right to be paid for time off for elective surgery. Any payment of salary made by the Company in such circumstances is done so in its absolute discretion.] [Time off for elective surgery will be paid at your normal rate of pay.]

[If you wish to apply for time off for elective surgery, you should apply in writing as far in advance as possible of the day on which the surgery is to take place to . . . . (*insert name of contact*) stating the period of leave requested and the reasons for it. Any information provided will be maintained in strict confidence and will only be disclosed on a "need-to-know" basis. You may also be required to provide an appointment card and/or a statement from a qualified medical practitioner that elective surgery has been approved and confirming the time off required for recovery.]]

[Gender reassignment

Gender reassignment is a process which is undertaken under medical supervision for the purpose of reassigning a person's sex by changing physiological or other characteristics of sex, and it includes any part of such a process.

If required, the Company will grant you up to……. (*insert number*) days' leave in any one calendar year to undergo gender reassignment surgery. Medical appointments in connection with the gender reassignment process will be treated no less favourably than any other medical appointments. You should try to arrange medical appointments and surgery at times that will cause the minimum amount of inconvenience to the Company. If you require further time off, you may use your existing paid annual leave entitlement, provided you comply with the provisions relating to annual leave set out in your contract of employment and in the section on "Holidays".

[You have no contractual or statutory right to be paid for time off for gender reassignment medical appointments or surgery. Any payment of salary made by the Company in such circumstances is done so in its absolute discretion.] [Time off for gender reassignment [medical appointments and] surgery will be paid at your normal rate of pay.]

If you wish to apply for time off for gender reassignment surgery, you should apply in writing as far in advance as possible of the days on which time off is required to ………… (*insert name of contact*) stating the period of leave requested. Time off to attend medical appointments must be authorised by your line manager in advance in the normal way. Any information provided will be maintained in strict confidence and will only be disclosed on a "need-to-know" basis. You may also be required to provide an appointment card and/or a statement from a qualified medical practitioner that the process of gender reassignment has been approved and confirming the time off required after surgery.]

[Fertility treatment

If required, the Company will grant you up to ………... (*insert number*) days' leave in any one calendar year to undergo fertility treatment. Medical appointments in connection with the early stages of the fertility treatment process will be treated no less favourably than any other medical appointments. You should try to arrange fertility treatment at a time that will cause the minimum amount of inconvenience to the Company. If you require further time off, you may use your existing paid annual leave entitlement, provided you comply with the provisions relating to annual leave set out in your contract of employment and in the section on "Holidays".

[You have no contractual or statutory right to be paid for time off for fertility treatment. Any payment of salary made by the Company in such circumstances is done so in its absolute discretion.] [Time off for fertility treatment will be paid at your normal rate of pay.]

If you wish to apply for time off for fertility treatment, you should apply in writing as far in advance as possible of the days on which time off is required to . . . . . . (*insert name of contact*) stating the period of leave requested. Time off to attend medical appointments must be authorised by your line manager in advance in the normal way. Any information provided will be maintained in strict confidence and will only be disclosed on a "need-to-know" basis. You may also be required to provide an appointment card and/or a statement from a qualified medical practitioner that fertility treatment has been approved.]

[Voluntary reduced working hours

It is the Company's policy that employees may request a contractual reduction in their normal hours of work on a temporary basis, or alternatively the Company may ask an employee to agree to contractually reduce their normal hours of work for a defined temporary period of time.

An employee may wish to work shorter hours for a temporary period for a variety of purposes, such as to undergo a college or university course, on account of family responsibilities such as caring for a sick relative, to allow them to pursue a personal hobby or interest, to undertake voluntary/charity work or for any other purpose agreed with the Company.

The Company may also wish to ask an employee to work reduced hours for a defined temporary period of time if there is a downturn in business or in order to avoid redundancies.

This policy covers voluntary requests for reduced working hours for defined temporary periods only. Employees who wish to reduce their hours on a permanent basis should apply under the terms of the Company's Flexible Working Policy.

Reduced working hours will normally only be permitted for a maximum of . . . . (*insert number*) (weeks/months).

The Company will not impose reduced working hours on you under the terms of this policy without your agreement. Likewise, this policy does not give you the right to demand reduced working hours. Any change to your hours of work as set out in your contract of employment will be implemented only where both you and the Company agree.

Where there is an agreement to reduce your normal hours of work for a defined temporary period, this will be confirmed to you in writing by way of a change to your contract of employment. The written confirmation will state the new hours to be worked, the start and end date of the agreed variation to your contract (i.e. the period during which the reduced working hours will apply) and any consequent changes to the other terms of your contract, such as the relevant pro rata reduction in your salary and annual leave entitlement.

At the end of the agreed period, you will automatically revert to your previous working hours and pattern and the previous terms of your contract of employment, such as those related to salary and annual leave entitlement.]

General

Failure to return from leave and report for work on the due date of return without reasonable excuse is a disciplinary offence and will be dealt with in accordance with the Company's disciplinary procedure.

LETTER DECLINING A REFERENCE

.... *(insert address)*

....

....

.... *(insert date)*

Dear .... *(insert name)*

Re: Reference request for .... *(insert name of ex-employee)*

We write further to your letter dated .... *(insert date)* asking us to provide a reference in respect of the above named individual.

Unfortunately, after careful consideration we must advise you that we are not able to assist you on this occasion or, indeed, provide the information that you request.

Yours sincerely

.... *(insert name and signature)*

For and on behalf of the Company

LIST OF GROSS MISCONDUCT OFFENCES

For gross misconduct, the Company reserves the right to summarily dismiss an employee and normally dismissal will be without notice with pay only up to the point of dismissal.

Examples of gross misconduct, where the Company has reasonable grounds for believing that the following matters have occurred, are:

- dishonesty, theft or fraud

- communicating confidential information to third parties

- working for a competitor without permission

- falsification of company records or unauthorised removal or sale of Company products or property

- wilful damage to Company property

- conviction of a serious criminal offence (taking into account the provisions of the Rehabilitation of Offenders Act 1974)

- taking bribes in connection with employment

- actions which endanger an employee's safety

- knowingly breaking a legal requirement in connection with employment

- assault or threatening, inflammatory behaviour or rudeness to customers

- gross insubordination

- wilful refusal to carry out reasonable and proper requests

- false expense claims for fraudulent purposes

- being under the influence of alcohol or illegal drugs during working hours or on company property

- harassing or victimising another employee on the grounds of race, colour, ethnic origin, nationality, national origin, religion or belief, sex, sexual orientation, gender reassignment marital or civil partnership status, age or disability

- unauthorised absence

- bringing the Company into disrepute.

Note. This list is not exhaustive and can be added to suit the particular needs of each employer

MATERNITY LEAVE PLAN

This plan covers your statutory rights to maternity leave and Statutory Maternity Pay (SMP). You do not have to fill in this plan to benefit from the right to maternity leave and SMP, but you do have to give the Company most of the information it contains. You may therefore wish to use this plan as a straightforward way of making sure you give the Company all the necessary information so that you can take maternity leave and receive SMP if you qualify for it. Once you have completed the plan, you should immediately forward it to . . . . *(insert name of contact)* and you should keep a copy for your own records.

Telling the Company that you are pregnant

You can tell us that you are pregnant as soon as you want to. This can be before you have decided when to take maternity leave. You will, of course, need to tell us if you want to take paid time off for antenatal appointments. The latest date you can inform us of your pregnancy is the 15th week before your expected week of childbirth (EWC).

Telling the Company when you want to take maternity leave

You must have told us by the 15th week before your EWC when you want to start your maternity leave and begin to receive SMP. This should be in writing. If you are using this plan for this purpose, you need to give it to us at the latest during the 15th week before your EWC. If you later wish to change the date on which you will start your maternity leave, you must give us at least 28 days' advance notice of your proposed revised start date.

Statutory Maternity Pay (SMP)

As well as qualifying for maternity leave, you may also qualify for SMP. If you do not qualify for SMP, you may be able to claim Maternity Allowance (MA) from your local Jobcentre Plus.

How to use the plan

The plan is in three parts. Complete Part A first, followed by Part B. Use Part C only if you wish to return to work before you have taken your full maternity leave entitlement. Brief notes are given in the right hand column.

PART A - PLANNING MATERNITY LEAVE

I am giving you this form to let you know that I am pregnant and to notify you of when I want to start my maternity leave.

1. Your name:	
2. The Company's name:	
3. I am pregnant YES/NO* *(*delete as appropriate)*	**3.** See the notes above about telling the Company that you are pregnant.
4. My baby is due in the week beginning: Sunday . . . . *(insert date of expected week of childbirth)*	**4.** The expected week of childbirth is the week, beginning Sunday, in which it is expected you will have your baby.
5. A certificate confirming this: • has been given to you already. • is enclosed with this form. • will be given to you shortly.	**5.** If you qualify for SMP, you should advise us at least 28 days before you want to start to be paid. You should also provide a MAT B1 certificate, which your doctor or midwife will give you, to confirm you are pregnant and the date the baby is due within 21 days from the start of your SMP pay period. We cannot accept this certificate if your midwife or doctor signs it more than 20 weeks before your baby is due. If you do not qualify for SMP, you do not have to give us a MAT B1 certificate unless we ask for one.

PART B - MATERNITY LEAVE

1. I intend to start my maternity leave on: . . . . *(insert date)* My maternity leave will run for up to 52 weeks.	**1.** Start date: it is your decision when you start your maternity leave, but you cannot start it earlier than the eleventh week before your EWC. You must notify us of your intended start date in the 15th week before the EWC.
2. My maternity leave will finish on: . . . . (insert date)	**2.** End of maternity leave: this is the end of the 52nd week from when you start your maternity leave.

3. I am due back to work on: . . . . *(insert date)* I understand that if I want to return to work before this date, I must give you eight weeks' advance notice of the date on which I want to return.	**3.** Date due back to work: you are due back to work on the next working day after your maternity leave finishes.

You should now sign the plan.

Signed:. . . . . *(insert name of employee)*

Date:. . . . .

PART C - RETURNING TO WORK EARLY

You will be expected back at the end of your full maternity leave entitlement. You are due back on the date you put for question 3 of Part B. If you want to return earlier, you must give the Company at least eight weeks' advance notice. This does not have to be in writing, but you may like to use this part of the plan to let us know.

I intend to return to work before the end of my maternity leave. I intend to return to work on:. . . . . *(insert date)*

You should now sign below and send Part C to the Company.

Signed:. . . . . *(insert name of employee)*

Date:. . . . .

MATERNITY POLICY

Introduction

This section sets out the statutory rights and responsibilities of employees who are pregnant or have recently given birth and covers the arrangements for ante-natal care, pregnancy-related illness, maternity leave and pay. The Company implements the maternity rights set out in legislation.

The following abbreviations are used in this section:

EWC   Expected Week of Childbirth - the week, starting on a Sunday, in which your doctor or midwife expects you to give birth.

SMP   Statutory Maternity Pay.

QW   The Qualifying Week for SMP - the 15th week before the EWC.

Maternity rights

You have the following key maternity rights:

- time off for ante-natal care
- maternity pay - linked to your level of earnings
- maternity leave.

Notification of pregnancy

On becoming pregnant, you should notify your line manager as soon as you feel able to do so. This is important because there are health and safety considerations for the Company.

By the end of the Qualifying Week, or as soon as reasonably practicable afterwards, you are required to provide the following information in writing to the Company:

- that you are pregnant
- your EWC
- the date on which you intend to start your maternity leave.

In addition, you will need to provide your line manager with a MATB1 certificate. The MATB1 is issued by your doctor or midwife and it states when your baby is due. The certificate must have either your doctor's name and address on it, or if issued by a midwife, her name and registration number.

You are permitted to bring forward your maternity leave start date, provided you advise the Company in writing at least 28 days before the new start date or, if that is not possible, as soon as reasonably practicable. You may also postpone your maternity leave start date, provided you advise the Company in writing at least 28 days before the original proposed start date or, if that is not possible, as soon as reasonably practicable.

The Company will formally respond in writing to your notification of your leave plans within 28 days, confirming the date on which you are expected to return to work if you take your full 52-week entitlement to maternity leave.

Time off for ante-natal care

Once you have advised the Company that you are pregnant, you are entitled to take reasonable time off work with pay to attend the ante-natal clinic and other ante-natal appointments made on the advice of your doctor, registered midwife or registered health visitor. Ante-natal care may include relaxation and parent craft classes that your doctor, midwife or health visitor has advised you to attend, as well as medical examinations.

In order to be entitled to take time off for ante-natal care, you are required to produce a medical certificate from one of the above, stating that you are pregnant. Except in the case of your first appointment, you should also produce evidence of the appointment, such as an appointment card, to your line manager. You must endeavour to give your line manager as much advance notice as possible of ante-natal appointments and you should try to arrange them as close to the start or the end of your working day as possible.

Health and safety

The Company has a duty to take care of the health and safety of all employees. We are also required to carry out a risk assessment which may include assessing the workplace risks to women who are pregnant, have recently given birth or are breastfeeding where the work is of a kind which could involve a risk of harm or danger to their health and safety or the health and safety of their baby and the risk arises from either processes, working conditions or physical, chemical or biological agents in the workplace. If applicable, the Company will provide you with information as to any risks identified in any risk assessment. If the risk assessment reveals that you would be exposed to health hazards in carrying out your normal job duties, the Company will take such steps as are reasonably necessary to avoid those risks, such as altering your working conditions. In some cases, this may mean offering you suitable alternative work (if available) on terms and conditions which are not substantially less favourable.

If it is not possible for the Company to alter your working conditions to remove the risks to your health and there is no suitable alternative work available to offer you on a temporary basis, the Company may suspend you from work on maternity grounds until such time as there are no longer any risks to your health. This may be for the remainder of your pregnancy until the commencement of your maternity leave. If you are suspended in these circumstances, your employment will continue during the period of the suspension and it does not in any way affect your statutory or contractual employment and maternity rights.

Sickness absence

If you are absent from work during your pregnancy due to sickness, you will receive sick pay in the same manner as any other sickness absence provided that you have not yet begun ordinary maternity leave. If, however, you are absent from work due to a pregnancy-related illness after the beginning of the 4th week before the EWC but before the date you have notified, or before you have notified a date, on which you intend to commence your maternity leave, then your maternity leave will usually begin automatically on the day after the first day of your absence. You must notify the Company that you are absent from work wholly or partly because of pregnancy as soon as is reasonably practicable and, until your maternity leave commences, you are still required to comply with the reporting procedure set out in the section on Sickness Absence.

Maternity leave

All pregnant employees are entitled to take up to 26 weeks' ordinary maternity leave and up to 26 weeks' additional maternity leave, making a total of 52 weeks. This is regardless of the number of hours worked or length of service. Additional maternity leave begins on the day after ordinary maternity leave ends.

Ordinary maternity leave can start at any time after the beginning of the eleventh week before your EWC (unless your child is born prematurely before that date). Maternity leave will start on whichever date is the earlier of:

- your chosen start date

- the day after you give birth

- the day after any day on which you are absent for a pregnancy-related reason in the four weeks before the EWC.

If you give birth before your maternity leave was due to start, you must notify the Company in writing of the date of the birth as soon as reasonably practicable.

The law requires all employees to take a minimum of two weeks of compulsory maternity leave immediately after the birth of their child (four weeks for factory workers).

Ordinary maternity leave

During the period of ordinary maternity leave, your contract of employment continues in force and you are entitled to receive all your contractual benefits, except for salary. In particular, any benefits in kind will continue, annual leave entitlement will continue to accrue and pension contributions will continue to be made. Your pension contributions will be based on your actual pay whilst the Company's contributions will be based on the salary you would have received had you not gone on maternity leave.

Salary will be replaced by statutory maternity pay (SMP) if you are eligible to receive it. On resuming work after maternity leave, you will be entitled to benefit from any general pay increases that may have been awarded in your absence.

You should endeavour to take any outstanding annual leave that may be due to you before the commencement of your ordinary maternity leave. You are reminded that holiday must be taken in the year that it is earned and therefore if the holiday year is due to end during maternity leave, you should take the full year's entitlement before starting your maternity leave: see the section on Holidays for further information.

Additional maternity leave

During the period of additional maternity leave, your contract of employment continues in force and, as is the case during the period of ordinary maternity leave, you are entitled to receive all your contractual benefits, except for salary. Any benefits in kind will continue and annual leave entitlement will continue to accrue.

Salary will be replaced by statutory maternity pay (SMP) for the first 13 weeks of additional maternity leave if you are eligible to receive it. The remaining 13 weeks of additional maternity leave will be unpaid.

Pension contributions will continue to be made during the period when you are receiving SMP but not during any period of unpaid additional maternity leave.

Statutory maternity pay

SMP is payable for up to 39 weeks during your maternity leave. You are entitled to SMP if:

- you have been continuously employed by the Company for at least 26 weeks at the end of the QW and you are still employed during that week

- your average weekly earnings in the eight weeks up to and including the QW are not less than the lower earnings limit for National Insurance contributions

- you are still pregnant eleven weeks before the start of your EWC (or have already given birth)

- you provide a MAT B1 certificate stating your EWC

- you give the Company proper notification of your pregnancy in accordance with the rules set out above.

For the first six weeks, SMP is paid at the higher rate, which is equivalent to 90% of your average weekly earnings calculated over the period of eight weeks up to and including the QW. For the purpose of calculating average weekly earnings, shift allowances, on-call allowance, over-time payments, bonuses and commission are all included.

The standard rate of SMP is paid for the remaining 33 weeks (or less if you decide to return to work sooner). This is paid at a rate set by the Government for the relevant tax year, or 90% of your average weekly earnings calculated over the period of eight weeks up to and including the QW if this is lower than the Government's set weekly rate.

If you become eligible for a pay rise between the start of the original calculation period and the end of your maternity leave (whether ordinary or additional maternity leave), the higher or standard rate of SMP will be re-calculated to take account of your pay rise, regardless of whether SMP has already been paid. This means your SMP will be re-calculated and increased retrospectively, or that you may qualify for SMP if you did not previously. You will be paid a lump sum to make up any difference between SMP already paid and the amount payable as a result of the pay rise.

SMP is paid into your bank account in the same way as salary is normally paid.

SMP is treated as earnings and is therefore subject to income tax and National Insurance deductions.

Payment of SMP cannot start prior to the eleventh week before your EWC. SMP can start from any day of the week in accordance with the date you start your maternity leave.

SMP is payable whether or not you intend to return to work after your maternity leave.

It is important for maternity pay purposes that you notify your line manager if, during the maternity pay period, you are taken into legal custody or start to work for another employer.

If you have been working for the Company for less than 26 weeks at the QW, you are not eligible to receive SMP. You may, however, be able to apply to the Department of Work and Pensions for Maternity Allowance if you meet their qualifying conditions.

Contact during maternity leave

Shortly before your maternity leave starts, the Company will discuss the arrangements for you to keep in touch during your leave, should you wish to do so. The Company reserves the right in any event to maintain reasonable contact with you from time to time during your maternity leave. This may be to discuss your plans for return to work, to discuss any special arrangements to be made or training to be given to ease your return to work or simply to update you on developments at work during your absence.

Keeping in touch days

Except during the first two weeks from childbirth, you may agree to work for the Company for up to a maximum of ten days during either your ordinary or additional maternity leave without that work bringing the period of your maternity leave to an end and without loss of a week's SMP. These are known as "keeping in touch" days. Any work carried out on a day shall constitute a day's work for these purposes.

The Company has no right to require you to carry out any work, and you have no right to undertake any work, during your maternity leave. Any work undertaken, including the amount of salary paid for any work done on keeping in touch days, is entirely a matter for agreement between the Company and you. Any keeping in touch days worked do not extend the period of your maternity leave. Once the keeping in touch days have been used up, you will lose a week's SMP for any week in which you agree to work for the Company.

Returning to work

You will have been formally advised in writing by the Company of the date on which your maternity leave will end and the date on which you are expected to return to work if you take your full 52-week entitlement to maternity leave. You are expected to return on this date, unless you notify the Company otherwise. If you are unable to attend work at the end of your maternity leave due to sickness or injury, the Company's normal arrangements for sickness absence will apply. In any other case, late return without prior authorisation will be treated as unauthorised absence.

Whilst you are under no obligation to do so, it would assist the Company if you could confirm as soon as convenient during your maternity leave that you will be returning to work as expected.

If you wish to return to work earlier than your expected return date, you must give the Company, preferably in writing, at least eight weeks' notice of your proposed date of early return. If you fail to do so, the Company may postpone your return to such a date as will give the Company eight weeks' notice, provided that this is not later than your expected return date.

If you decide not to return to work at all after maternity leave, you must give notice of resignation as soon as possible and in accordance with the terms of your contract of employment. If the notice period would expire after your maternity leave has ended, the Company may require you to return to work for the remainder of your notice period.

Your rights on return to work

On resuming work after ordinary maternity leave, you are entitled to return to the same job as you occupied before commencing maternity leave on the same terms and conditions of employment as if you had not been absent. On resuming work after additional maternity leave, again you are entitled to return to the same job as you occupied before commencing maternity leave on the same terms and conditions as if you had not been absent. If, however, there is some reason why it is not reasonably practicable for the Company to take you back in your original job, you will be offered suitable alternative work of equivalent status and responsibility and on terms and conditions that are no less favourable than would have applied if you had not been absent.

If you are a full-time employee, you have no automatic right to return to work on a part-time basis or to make other changes to your working patterns at the end of your maternity leave. However, all requests for part-time work or other flexible working arrangements will be considered in line with the operational requirements of the Company's business. It is the Company's policy to promote flexible working arrangements for all employees and in particular for women returning from maternity leave. Further details, including the procedure to be followed, can be found in the section on Flexible Working. If you would like this option to be considered, you should write to your line manager setting out your proposals as far in advance of your return date as possible, so that there is adequate time for full consideration of your request.

MOBILITY AND RELOCATION CLAUSE

Your normal place of work is at . . . . *(insert address)*, provided that:

1. The Company reserves the right to require you to work at any other establishment or place of business of the Company (or of its associated companies or any of its or their customers, clients, contractors or suppliers), whether current or future, within (the United Kingdom/a radius of . . . . *(insert number)* miles from your normal place of work/reasonable daily commuting distance of your home) on a temporary basis according to the needs of the Company's business.

2. Where you are required to work somewhere other than your normal place of work on a temporary basis, the Company will endeavour to give you some prior written notice of the move but, depending on the particular circumstances, it may not always be possible to do so.

3. The Company also reserves the right to require you to work at any other establishment or place of business of the Company (or of its associated companies), whether current or future, within (the United Kingdom/a radius of . . . . *(insert number)* miles from your normal place of work/reasonable daily commuting distance of your home) on a permanent basis, again according to the needs of the Company's business.

4. Where you are required to move on a permanent basis, this will change your normal place of work and the Company will you give . . . . *(insert number)* weeks' prior written notice of the move.

5. Where any new normal place of work is not within (a . . . . *(insert number)* mile radius of your previous normal place of work/reasonable daily commuting distance of your home), you agree to relocate your home within . . . . *(insert number)* months of the relocation of your normal place of work to a residence which is within (a . . . . *(insert number)* mile radius of your new normal place of work/reasonable daily commuting distance of your new normal place of work).

6. The payment of any relocation expenses is subject to the provisions of the Company's Relocation Policy for the time being in force.

7. During the continuance of your employment with the Company, you must reside within a radius of . . . . *(insert number)* miles from your normal place of work.

PARENTAL LEAVE POLICY

This section sets out the Company's policy on parental leave. The Company implements the parental leave rights set out in legislation. Parental leave is additional to paternity leave, maternity leave, adoption leave and time off to deal with family emergencies.

Entitlement to parental leave

All periods of parental leave are unpaid. There is no contractual or statutory entitlement to be paid for absences relating to parental leave. Any payment of salary during parental leave is made at the absolute discretion of the Company.

Both mothers and fathers can take parental leave.

In order to qualify for parental leave, you must have worked for the Company for a continuous period of one year by the time you want to take the leave. If you have already taken part of your parental leave with a previous employer, you will not be able to take any further parental leave until you have completed one year's continuous employment with the Company.

You are entitled to take up to 13 weeks' parental leave in order to care for a natural or an adopted child (or to make arrangements for the child's welfare) if you meet one of the following eligibility conditions:

- you are the natural parent of or you have acquired formal parental responsibility for a child who is under five years old
- you have adopted a child under the age of 18.

In the case of birth fathers, you must be named on the child's birth certificate.

If you are the parent or adoptive parent of a disabled child who has been awarded Disability Living Allowance, you are entitled to take up to 18 weeks' parental leave.

When parental leave may be taken

Assuming you are eligible, you can choose to take parental leave:

- up until the child's fifth birthday
- in adoption cases, within five years after the child is first placed with you for adoption (or until the child's 18th birthday if that comes sooner)
- in the case of a child with a disability, up until the child's 18th birthday.

Taking time off for parental leave

Parental leave is for each child, so in the case of twins, 13 weeks' leave may be taken for each child. You must take parental leave in blocks of one week. If you take parental leave for a shorter period than one week (for example, two days), that will constitute a week's leave for the purpose of calculating your 13 weeks' parental leave entitlement (although you will continue to be paid as normal for the time you work). The exception to this is that parents of disabled children can take leave in blocks of one day.

A maximum of four weeks' parental leave can be taken in respect of any child during any one calendar year. Each parent is entitled to parental leave.

Procedure for notifying a request to take parental leave

You are required to give at least 21 days' written notice to your line manager of your proposed parental leave dates. If leave is to be taken immediately after birth or adoption, 21 days' written notice of the expected week of childbirth or the expected week of placement for adoption should be given. You must specify the dates on which your period of parental leave is to start and finish. A Parental Leave Request Form can be obtained from . . . . (insert name of contact). If it is not reasonably practicable for you to comply with the 21 days' notice requirement, you should give notice as soon as reasonably practicable. If you give notice that you wish your leave to start on the date of birth or adoption and that date is sooner or later than expected, your leave will begin on the actual date of birth or adoption.

At the time of requesting parental leave, you should:

- provide the name of the child in respect of whom you wish to take leave, stating their date of birth and your relationship to them

- produce an appropriate birth or adoption certificate or such other documentation as the Company may reasonably request

- produce evidence of your child's entitlement to Disability Living Allowance (where relevant)

- specify parental leave as the reason for absence

- declare any periods of parental leave you have taken with a previous employer.

Periods of parental leave with previous employers

The period of 13 weeks' leave (or 18 weeks' leave where Disability Living Allowance applies) is the maximum you can take and periods of leave taken with a previous employer will be taken into account when calculating this period. The Company will expect you to declare periods of leave with a previous employer either before or at the time of making a request for parental leave. The Company may also check with your previous employer how much parental leave you have taken at your previous employment.

Postponement of parental leave

The Company reserves the right to postpone a period of parental leave for up to six months where it considers the operation of its business would be unduly disrupted if the leave were to be taken at the time requested. For example, leave may be postponed during particularly busy periods, seasonal peaks or where a significant proportion of your department have already applied to be absent from work at the same time.

The Company will confirm any postponement arrangements in writing no later than seven days after receipt of your request to take parental leave. This letter will state the reason for postponement and set out the proposed new dates of parental leave. The Company will attempt to agree with you a suitable alternative date when the parental leave can commence.

The Company will not postpone leave if you have given notice to take it immediately after the time the child is born or is placed with you for adoption.

Rights during parental leave

During parental leave your contract of employment continues. You are entitled to all of your statutory employment benefits, but some contractual benefits can be suspended by the Company. For example, you will continue to accrue your statutory annual leave entitlement during parental leave but you do not have the right to accrue any additional contractual annual leave entitlement.

Your seniority, pension rights and rights to any other service-related benefits are unaffected by parental leave.

Right to return to work after parental leave

At the end of parental leave, you will be entitled to return to the same job on the same terms and conditions as if you had not been absent, provided always that your period of parental leave was for a period of four weeks or less and that you have not taken parental leave immediately after taking additional maternity leave or additional adoption leave.

Where your period of parental leave is taken immediately after taking additional maternity leave or additional adoption leave or your parental leave period is more than four weeks, again you will be entitled to return to the same job on the same terms and conditions as if you had not been absent. If, however, there is some reason why it is not reasonably practicable for the Company to take you back in your original job, you will be offered suitable alternative work of equivalent status and responsibility and on terms and conditions that are no less favourable than would have applied if you had not been absent.

Claiming parental leave dishonestly

If you act dishonestly in claiming an entitlement to parental leave, this is a disciplinary offence and will be dealt with under the Company's disciplinary procedure. This includes attempting to claim leave for a child who is too old, claiming leave for purposes other than caring for a child or misleading the Company about parental leave taken with a previous employer. Depending on the seriousness of the offence, it may amount to potential gross misconduct and could result in your summary dismissal.

PATERNITY LEAVE POLICY

The Company implements the paternity leave rights set out in legislation. Paternity leave is additional to both parental leave and time off to deal with family emergencies (see the sections on Parental Leave and Time Off for Dependants). It is also additional to paid annual leave entitlement.

In order to qualify for the right to take paternity leave, you must have worked for the Company for a continuous period of 26 weeks by the week that falls 15 weeks before the week in which the child is expected to be born. In respect of an adopted child, the period is calculated as at the week in which the child's adopter is notified of having been matched with the child for adoption. You must also meet each of the following eligibility criteria:

• you have, or expect to have, responsibility for the upbringing of the child

• you are either the biological father or adopter of the child or you are married to or the cohabiting partner of the child's mother or adopter

• you are making the request to help care for the child or support the child's mother.

Assuming you are eligible, you are able to take up to two weeks' paid paternity leave. You can take this in a single block of either one or two weeks. Odd days cannot be taken. Paternity leave can start either from the date the child is born or from a chosen number of days or weeks after the date of childbirth (or, in respect of an adopted child, from the date of placing for adoption). It can start on any day of the week, but it must be completed within eight weeks of the date of childbirth (or date of placement for adoption). If the child is born early, it must be completed within the period from the date of childbirth up to eight weeks after the expected date of childbirth.

In the case of multiple births, for example, twins, note that only one period of paternity leave is available.

During paternity leave, most employees will be entitled to Statutory Paternity Pay (SPP). The weekly rate of SPP is set by the Government for the relevant tax year, or it is 90% of your average weekly earnings if this is lower than the Government's set weekly rate.

Employees whose average weekly earnings are less than the lower earnings limit for National Insurance contributions are not eligible to receive SPP.

SPP is treated as earnings and is therefore subject to PAYE and National Insurance deductions.

If you wish to request to take paternity leave, you must inform your line manager in writing of your request no later than the 15th week before the expected week of childbirth. You must provide written details of when the child is due, whether you wish to take one or two weeks' paternity leave and when you want your paternity leave to start. A Paternity Leave Request Form can be obtained from . . . . *(insert name of contact).*

In the case of an adopted child, you must give written notice of your intention to take paternity leave no later than seven days after the date on which notification of the match with the child is given by the adoption agency. The notice must specify the date on which the adopter was notified of having been matched with the child, the date the child is expected to be placed for adoption, whether you wish to take one or two weeks' paternity leave and when you want your paternity leave to start.

You are able to change your mind about the date on which you want your paternity leave to start provided you give at least 28 days' written notice of the new date to your line manager.

PAY IN LIEU OF NOTICE CLAUSE

The Company reserves the right to make a payment in lieu of notice for all or any part of your notice period on the termination of your employment. This provision, which is at the Company's absolute discretion, applies whether notice to terminate the contract is given by you or the Company. Any such payment will consist solely of basic salary (as at the date of termination) and shall be subject to such deductions of income tax and National Insurance contributions as the Company is required or authorised to make.

For the avoidance of doubt, the payment in lieu of notice shall not include any element relating to:

- any bonus or commission payments that might otherwise have been due during the period for which the payment in lieu is made

- any payment in respect of benefits which you would have been entitled to receive during the period for which the payment in lieu is made; and

- any payment in respect of any annual leave entitlement that would have accrued during the period for which the payment in lieu is made.

[The Company may pay any sums due under this clause in equal monthly instalments until the date end of the period for which the payment in lieu is made.]

You have no right to receive a payment in lieu of notice unless the Company exercises its discretion under this clause.

RECRUITMENT POLICY

It is the Company's policy that line managers and the Human Resources department are jointly responsible for the recruitment of new employees. Line managers should always keep the senior management of the Company up-to-date regarding future recruitment intentions. Where there is a need to recruit a new employee into the Company, the following procedure should be followed:

The line manager should first complete a Recruitment Authorisation Form (copy attached) and ensure it is discussed with and signed off by a director of the Company. This form requires a justification for the post as well as:

- an up-to-date job description and a person specification

- financial implications

- advertisement wording and medium for publication

- estimated costs of advertising the post.

The line manager should first consider and discuss with the Human Resources department the most appropriate place(s) to post the vacancy or whether an approved employment agency should be used.

Where recruitment is planned to fill a vacancy created by a leaver (other than on redundancy grounds), approval will normally be granted automatically. If the post is new or upgraded, the director will need to be satisfied that it can be justified.

The form must then be forwarded to the Human Resources department for approval. If approved, they will deal with the necessary recruitment administration, including placing advertisements, arranging interviews, etc.

Selection of candidates for interview must be decided jointly by the line manager and the Human Resources department. Shortlisting, interviewing and selection must always be carried out without regard to gender, marital status, sexual orientation, race, colour, nationality or ethnic or national origins, religion or belief or age. However, line managers may decline to recruit applicants who are over the Company's normal retirement age where this is 65 or above and applicants who are within six months of this age as at the date of their application. Any applicant who has a disability must not be excluded unless it is clear that the applicant does not meet the minimum criteria outlined in the person specification and they would still fail to do so even if reasonable adjustments were made to work provisions, criteria or practices. Reasonable adjustments should also be made to the recruitment process to ensure that no applicant is disadvantaged because of their disability.

All interviews must be conducted by the line manager and at least one other line manager or member of the Human Resources department.

All offers of employment, whether written or verbal, must have the prior approval of a director of the Company.

It is the Company's policy that all vacancies will be advertised internally (by e-mail/posting on notice boards) as well as externally and existing employees are to be encouraged to apply for vacant posts if they have the requisite skills, qualifications and experience.

The Company aims at all times to recruit the person who is most suited to the particular post. Recruitment must be solely on the basis of the applicant's abilities, qualifications, experience and merit as measured against the job description and person specification. The guidelines promulgated in the Company's equal opportunities statement must be followed at all stages of recruitment and selection. Line managers conducting recruitment interviews must ensure that questions asked of job applicants are in no way discriminatory or personally intrusive. The interview should focus on the needs of the post and the skills, qualifications and experience needed to perform it effectively.

An interview record must be made and passed to the Human Resources department where it will be retained for a suitable period of time. On no account should a job offer be made during or at the end of an interview. Selection testing will be used as part of the recruitment process only with the prior approval of the Human Resources department. Any test used must have been validated in relation to the post and be conducted by a suitably trained person.

It is the Company's policy to seek at least two written references, one of which must be from a previous employer (or, if this is the prospective employee's first job, their school teacher or higher or further education lecturer) and to ask for documentary proof of qualifications and eligibility to work in the UK. Any offer of employment must be conditional on this documentation being satisfactory to the Company. Before references are taken up, the prospective employee's consent should first be sought.

REDUNDANCY PAYMENTS READY RECKONER

To calculate the number of weeks' pay due, read off the employee's age and number of complete years' service.

The statutory maximum weekly pay figure is £380 from October 1 2009.

Our table assumes that the earliest age at which someone can start work is 14 and we have assumed a maximum age of 75. If an employee is made redundant beyond the age of 75, the same calculation would apply as that which applies to a 75-year old.

Age																			
16	1.0	-	-	-	-	-	-	-	-	-	-	-	-	-	-	-	-	-	-
17	1.0	1.5	-	-	-	-	-	-	-	-	-	-	-	-	-	-	-	-	-
18	1.0	1.5	2.0	-	-	-	-	-	-	-	-	-	-	-	-	-	-	-	-
19	1.0	1.5	2.0	2.5	-	-	-	-	-	-	-	-	-	-	-	-	-	-	-
20	1.0	1.5	2.0	2.5	3.0	-	-	-	-	-	-	-	-	-	-	-	-	-	-
21	1.0	1.5	2.0	2.5	3.0	3.5	-	-	-	-	-	-	-	-	-	-	-	-	-
22	1.0	1.5	2.0	2.5	3.0	3.5	4.0	-	-		-	-	-	-	-	-	-	-	-
23	1.5	2.0	2.5	3.0	3.5	4.0	4.5	5.0	-	-	-	-	-	-	-	-	-	-	-
24	2.0	2.5	3.0	3.5	4.0	4.5	5.0	5.5	6.0	-	-	-	-	-	-	-	-	-	-
25	2.0	3.0	3.5	4.0	4.5	5.0	5.5	6.0	6.5	7.0	-	-	-	-	-	-	-	-	-
26	2.0	3.0	4.0	4.5	5.0	5.5	6.0	6.5	7.0	7.5	8.0	-	-	-	-	-	-	-	-
27	2.0	3.0	4.0	5.0	5.5	6.0	6.5	7.0	7.5	8.0	8.5	9.0	-	-	-	-	-	-	-
28	2.0	3.0	4.0	5.0	6.0	6.5	7.0	7.5	8.0	8.5	9.0	9.5	10.0	-	-	-	-	-	-
29	2.0	3.0	4.0	5.0	6.0	7.0	7.5	8.0	8.5	9.0	9.5	10.0	10.5	11.0	-	-	-	-	-
30	2.0	3.0	4.0	5.0	6.0	7.0	8.0	8.5	9.0	9.5	10.0	10.5	11.0	11.5	12.0	-	-	-	-
31	2.0	3.0	4.0	5.0	6.0	7.0	8.0	9.0	9.5	10.0	10.5	11.0	11.5	12.0	12.5	13.0	-	-	-
32	2.0	3.0	4.0	5.0	6.0	7.0	8.0	9.0	10.0	10.5	11.0	11.5	12.0	12.5	13.0	13.5	14.0	-	-
33	2.0	3.0	4.0	5.0	6.0	7.0	8.0	9.0	10.0	11.0	11.5	12.0	12.5	13.0	13.5	14.0	14.5	15.0	-
34	2.0	3.0	4.0	5.0	6.0	7.0	8.0	9.0	10.0	11.0	12.0	12.5	13.0	13.5	14.0	14.5	15.0	15.5	16.0
35	2.0	3.0	4.0	5.0	6.0	7.0	8.0	9.0	10.0	11.0	12.0	13.0	13.5	14.0	14.5	15.0	15.5	16.0	16.0
36	2.0	3.0	4.0	5.0	6.0	7.0	8.0	9.0	10.0	11.0	12.0	13.0	14.0	14.5	15.0	15.5	16.0	16.5	17.0
37	2.0	3.0	4.0	5.0	6.0	7.0	8.0	9.0	10.0	11.0	12.0	13.0	14.0	15.0	15.5	16.0	16.5	17.0	17.5
38	2.0	3.0	4.0	5.0	6.0	7.0	8.0	9.0	10.0	11.0	12.0	13.0	14.0	15.0	16.0	16.5	17.0	17.5	18.0
39	2.0	3.0	4.0	5.0	6.0	7.0	8.0	9.0	10.0	11.0	12.0	13.0	14.0	15.0	16.0	17.0	17.5	18.0	18.5
40	2.0	3.0	4.0	5.0	6.0	7.0	8.0	9.0	10.0	11.0	12.0	13.0	14.0	15.0	16.0	17.0	18.0	18.5	19.0
41	2.0	3.0	4.0	5.0	6.0	7.0	8.0	9.0	10.0	11.0	12.0	13.0	14.0	15.0	16.0	17.0	18.0	19.0	19.5
42	2.5	3.5	4.5	5.5	6.5	7.5	8.5	9.5	10.5	11.5	12.5	13.5	14.5	15.5	16.5	17.5	18.5	19.5	20.5
43	3.0	4.0	5.0	6.0	7.0	8.0	9.0	10.0	11.0	12.0	13.0	14.0	15.0	16.0	17.0	18.0	19.0	20.0	21.0
44	3.0	4.5	5.5	6.5	7.5	8.5	9.5	10.5	11.5	12.5	13.5	14.5	15.5	16.5	17.5	18.5	19.5	20.5	21.5
45	3.0	4.5	6.0	7.0	8.0	9.0	10.0	11.0	12.0	13.0	14.0	15.0	16.0	17.0	18.0	19.0	20.0	21.0	22.0
46	3.0	4.5	6.0	7.5	8.5	9.5	10.5	11.5	12.5	13.5	14.5	15.5	16.5	17.5	18.5	19.5	20.5	21.5	22.5
47	3.0	4.5	6.0	7.5	9.0	10.0	11.0	12.0	13.0	14.0	15.0	16.0	17.0	18.0	19.0	20.0	21.0	22.0	23.0
48	3.0	4.5	6.0	7.5	9.0	10.5	11.5	12.5	13.5	14.5	15.5	16.5	17.5	18.5	19.5	20.5	21.5	22.5	23.5

49	3.0	4.5	6.0	7.5	9.0	10.5	12.0	13.0	14.0	15.0	16.0	17.0	18.0	19.0	20.0	21.0	22.0	23.0	24.0
50	3.0	4.5	6.0	7.5	9.0	10.5	12.0	13.5	14.5	15.5	16.5	17.5	18.5	19.5	20.5	21.5	22.5	23.5	24.5
51	3.0	4.5	6.0	7.5	9.0	10.5	12.0	13.5	15.0	16.0	17.0	18.0	19.0	20.0	21.0	22.0	23.0	24.0	25.0
52	3.0	4.5	6.0	7.5	9.0	10.5	12.0	13.5	15.0	16.5	17.5	18.5	19.5	20.5	21.5	22.5	23.5	24.5	25.5
53	3.0	4.5	6.0	7.5	9.0	10.5	12.0	13.5	15.0	16.5	18.0	19.0	20.0	21.0	22.0	23.0	24.0	25.0	26.0
54	3.0	4.5	6.0	7.5	9.0	10.5	12.0	13.5	15.0	16.5	18.0	19.5	20.5	21.5	22.5	23.5	24.5	25.5	26.5
55	3.0	4.5	6.0	7.5	9.0	10.5	12.0	13.5	15.0	16.5	18.0	19.5	21.0	22.0	23.0	24.0	25.0	26.0	27.0
56	3.0	4.5	6.0	7.5	9.0	10.5	12.0	13.5	15.0	16.5	18.0	19.5	21.0	22.5	23.5	24.5	25.5	26.5	27.5
57	3.0	4.5	6.0	7.5	9.0	10.5	12.0	13.5	15.0	16.5	18.0	19.5	21.0	22.5	24.0	25.0	26.0	27.0	28.0
58	3.0	4.5	6.0	7.5	9.0	10.5	12.0	13.5	15.0	16.5	18.0	19.5	21.0	22.5	24.0	25.5	26.5	27.5	28.5
59	3.0	4.5	6.0	7.5	9.0	10.5	12.0	13.5	15.0	16.5	18.0	19.5	21.0	22.5	24.0	25.5	27.0	28.0	29.0
60	3.0	4.5	6.0	7.5	9.0	10.5	12.0	13.5	15.0	16.5	18.0	19.5	21.0	22.5	24.0	25.5	27.0	28.5	29.5
61	3.0	4.5	6.0	7.	9.0	10.5	12.0	13.5	15.0	16.5	18.0	19.5	21.0	22.5	24.0	25.5	27.0	28.5	30.0
62	3.0	4.5	6.0	7.5	9.0	10.5	12.0	13.5	15.0	16.5	18.0	19.5	21.0	22.5	24.0	25.5	27.0	28.5	30.0
63	3.0	4.5	6.0	7.5	9.0	10.5	12.0	13.5	15.0	16.5	18.0	19.5	21.0	22.5	24.0	25.5	27.0	28.5	30.0
64	3.0	4.5	6.0	7.5	9.0	10.5	12.0	13.5	15.0	16.5	18.0	19.5	21.0	22.5	24.0	25.5	27.0	28.5	30.0
65	3.0	4.5	6.0	7.5	9.0	10.5	12.0	13.5	15.0	16.5	18.0	19.5	21.0	22.5	24.0	25.5	27.0	28.5	30.0
66	3.0	4.5	6.0	7.5	9.0	10.5	12.0	13.5	15.0	16.5	18.0	19.5	21.0	22.5	24.0	25.5	27.0	28.5	30.0
67	3.0	4.5	6.0	7.5	9.0	10.5	12.0	13.5	15.0	16.5	18.0	19.5	21.0	22.5	24.0	25.5	27.0	28.5	30.0
68	3.0	4.5	6.0	7.5	9.0	10.5	12.0	13.5	15.0	16.5	18.0	19.5	21.0	22.5	24.0	25.5	27.0	28.5	30.0
69	3.0	4.5	6.0	7.5	9.0	10.5	12.0	13.5	15.0	16.5	18.0	19.5	21.0	22.5	24.0	25.5	27.0	28.5	30.0
70	3.0	4.5	6.0	7.5	9.0	10.5	12.0	13.5	15.0	16.5	18.0	19.5	21.0	22.5	24.0	25.5	27.0	28.5	30.0
71	3.0	4.5	6.0	7.5	9.0	10.5	12.0	13.5	15.0	16.5	18.0	19.5	21.0	22.5	24.0	25.5	27.0	28.5	30.0
72	3.0	4.5	6.0	7.5	9.0	10.5	12.0	13.5	15.0	16.5	18.0	19.5	21.0	22.5	24.0	25.5	27.0	28.5	30.0
73	3.0	4.5	6.0	7.5	9.0	10.5	12.0	13.5	15.0	16.	18.0	19.5	21.0	22.5	24.0	25.5	27.0	28.5	30.0
4	3.0	4.5	6.0	7.5	9.0	10.5	12.0	13.5	15.0	16.5	18.0	19.5	21.0	22.5	24.0	25.5	27.0	28.5	30.0
75	3.0	4.5	6.0	7.5	9.0	10.5	12.0	13.5	15.0	16.5	18.0	19.5	21.0	22.5	24.0	25.5	27.0	28.5	30.0

REDUNDANCY POLICY

Avoiding redundancy

Should circumstances arise where redundancy may be a possibility because fewer employees are needed to perform the Company's work, the first steps the Company will take will be to:

- reduce overtime to a workable minimum

- restrict recruitment

- investigate measures such as short-time working and/or lay-offs

- investigate whether there are opportunities for redeployment to other departments within the Company

- explore other methods by which desired cost cuts could be achieved

- explore whether there are any other options available in order to avoid redundancy.

If redundancies cannot be avoided, the Company will give consideration to terminating agency workers and asking for volunteers. Whilst the Company will aim to keep the number of compulsory redundancies to a minimum, the overriding consideration will always be the future needs of the business.

Consultation and selection

If the need for compulsory redundancies arises, the selection of employees for redundancy will be in accordance with the section on "Selection Criteria" and there will be full consultation with employees throughout the redundancy selection process. Employees will be notified at the earliest possible opportunity of the reasons for the potential redundancy situation and of the Company's proposals.

The Company will carry out consultations over the following time periods:

- a minimum of 90 days' consultation where 100 or more jobs are proposed to be made redundant

- a minimum of 30 days' consultation where 20 or more jobs are proposed to be made redundant

- as much consultation as is reasonably practicable where fewer than 20 employees are proposed to be made redundant.

During the consultation exercise, full information will be provided to employees and/or their representatives about the Company's proposals and there will be adequate opportunity for employees or their representatives to respond. Information provided may include: the reasons for the proposed redundancies; the numbers and categories of employees who may be made redundant; the proposed method of selecting employees for redundancy; the proposed method of carrying out the redundancies, including the time period over which the dismissals may take effect; and the proposed method of calculating redundancy payments (if non-statutory).

The Company will also enter into individual consultation with each employee provisionally selected for redundancy. Each employee will have the right to be informed of the basis for their selection and be invited to put forward any representations, which the Company will fully consider before making a final decision on which employees are to be made redundant.

The chosen selection criteria will be fairly and consistently applied and will be capable of being backed up with evidence and/or data.

Voluntary redundancy

If the Company does ask for volunteers for redundancy, invitations will be offered to all employees whose jobs are at risk of redundancy. The opportunity to volunteer for redundancy will be available for a defined period only. Employees who choose to apply for voluntary redundancy are not guaranteed to have their application accepted. The Company has the absolute discretion to decide whether or not to accept an employee's application for voluntary redundancy.

Where an employee's application is provisionally accepted, they will be notified of this in writing. Employees who volunteer and are accepted for redundancy will be entitled to statutory redundancy pay in the same way as employees who are made compulsorily redundant. [However, at the Company's absolute discretion, employees who volunteer and are accepted for redundancy may be offered a redundancy payment that is higher than the level of redundancy pay payable to employees who are selected compulsorily.]

Alternative employment

Once provisional redundancy selections have been made, the Company will seek to identify any alternative vacancies that may be suitable.

The Company reserves the right to make the final decision as to whether or not to offer an available alternative position to a redundant employee. If a decision is made to offer a position, the offer will be made in writing. Where alternative employment is offered and accepted, it is the Company's policy to operate a trial period of four weeks in the new post. This is a statutory requirement. If it is established that the post is not objectively suitable for the employee, their employment will be terminated at the end of the trial period and the employee will still receive a statutory redundancy payment based on the date on which their original job ended. The Company reserves the right to make the final decision on termination of employment. An employee who unreasonably refuses an offer of suitable alternative employment (whether before, during or after the trial period) may forfeit their right to a statutory redundancy payment.

Redundancy pay

Redundant employees who have a minimum of two years' continuous employment with the Company will be entitled to be paid statutory redundancy pay, which is calculated according to the employee's age, length of service and gross weekly pay subject to a statutory maximum.

[Entirely on a discretionary basis, the Company may also offer an enhanced redundancy payment [that is based on the statutory redundancy payment calculation]. Any enhanced redundancy payments are paid wholly at the discretion of the Company and there is no contractual right for an employee to receive an enhanced redundancy payment at any time, regardless of whether or not enhanced redundancy payments have been paid to other redundant employees on previous occasions.]

Exclusions

Except in respect of any statutory collective consultation obligations on the Company, this redundancy policy does not apply to any employee who has been employed by the Company for less than one year.

This redundancy policy has no contractual force and should be regarded as providing guidelines only.

REFUSAL OF PARENTAL LEAVE REQUEST

To: . . . . *(insert name of employee)*

From: . . . . *(insert name of contact at the Company)*

I confirm that I have received your request for parental leave. Unfortunately, I must advise you that you are not eligible to take the period of parental leave requested because:

[You do not have sufficient service with the Company to qualify. At the date the proposed period of parental leave is to commence, you must have a minimum of one year's continuous employment with the Company.]*

[You have already exhausted your 13 weeks' entitlement to parental leave (or 18 weeks if the child is disabled) either with the Company or with a previous employer.]*

[You have already exhausted your four weeks' entitlement to parental leave within the last year.]*

[You have not given the Company a minimum of 21 days' notice prior to the requested start date.]*

[Your child is now over the age of five (or 18 if the child is disabled).]*

[You adopted your child more than five years ago or your adopted child is now over the age of 18.]*

[You have not complied with our request to provide evidence that you have, or expect to have, parental responsibility for a child under the age of five (or a disabled child under the age of 18) or an adopted child under the age of 18 who was adopted within the past five years.]*

(* delete as appropriate.)

If you have any questions about any aspect of your parental leave entitlement, please do not hesitate to get in touch with . . . . *(insert name of contact).*

Signed: . . . . *(insert name of employee)*

Date: . . . .

REIMBURSEMENT OF EXPENSES POLICY

Expenses incurred by employees will be reimbursed in accordance with these rules. These rules are designed to provide for the reimbursement of reasonable out-of-pocket expenses wholly, exclusively, necessarily and actually incurred by an employee engaged on the business of the Company.

In order to claim back expenses, you must complete and sign a claim form, have it countersigned by your line manager and then submit it to . . . . *(insert name of contact).* You are expected to provide original VAT receipts for expenditure incurred where this is reasonably practicable and you should give a full description of the expenditure incurred and why it was necessary. You should ensure all expense claims are made and submitted promptly.

The Company does not advance expenses.

Travelling expenses

The Company will reimburse travelling expenses necessarily incurred for business purposes. This is generally limited to the cost of travel from the Company's office to the business destination and return. Journeys between an employee's home and normal place of work are considered private and do not constitute business travel. Under no circumstances should you claim the cost of your journeys from home to your normal place of work.

The following expenses will be paid:

- where you use your own car, mileage allowance at a rate per mile as determined by the Company from time to time and notified to you. In this case, ensure you record your actual mileage undertaken. Your car must be comprehensively insured for use while on Company business

- where you have a Company car, the cost of fuel you have used in connection with Company business

- standard class rail or coach fares

- taxi fares where suitable public transport is not available

- economy class air fares (provided your line manager has authorised this in advance).

The Company is not responsible for any fines or penalty fares which you may receive while on Company business. The responsibility for paying such fines or penalties is yours.

Subsistence expenses

If you are required to stay away from home overnight on Company business, you may claim the costs of overnight accommodation (i.e. evening dinner, bed and breakfast only) at an appropriate hotel or guest house approved in advance by your line manager. The Company will not reimburse items of a personal nature such as alcoholic drinks, newspapers and private telephone calls.

If you are required to leave the office on Company business for more than . . . . *(insert number)* hours but you are not staying away overnight, day subsistence will be payable at rates determined by the Company from time to time and notified to you.

Telephone calls

The cost of telephone calls made using your private telephone or mobile phone, in connection with Company business, will be reimbursed. Itemised telephone bills are required to support this expense claim.

Staff and client entertainment

Only line managers are permitted to claim back expenses incurred for staff entertaining.

Client entertaining means hospitality provided by the Company or its employees to non-Company employees in connection with the business of the Company. You must judge what is reasonable in the circumstances and it should normally be possible for your line manager to agree to a level of entertaining expenditure before the commitments are made.

Other expenses

You should seek the prior approval of your line manager before incurring other expenses.

RESTRICTIVE COVENANTS CLAUSE

Note. Before inserting a restrictive covenant of any type into an employee's contract of employment, you must always consider whether it is really necessary to protect a legitimate business interest. If you do have a legitimate business interest to protect in relation to the particular employee, consider whether this can be achieved by a non-solicitation, non-dealing, non-poaching and/or a non-competition clause. Always remember that the shorter the duration of the covenant and the more limited it is in scope, the more likely it will be enforceable.

In order to protect the Company's interest in its goodwill and business connections, you hereby undertake that:

1. **Non-dealing.** You shall not at any time prior to the termination of your employment either on your own behalf or for any other person directly or indirectly approach, canvass, solicit or otherwise endeavour to entice away from the Company the custom of any person who is a customer, client or supplier of the Company and you shall not use your knowledge of or influence over any such customer, client or supplier to or for your own benefit or for the benefit of any other person carrying on business in competition with the Company or otherwise use your knowledge of or influence over any such customer, client or supplier to the detriment of the Company.

2. **Non-poaching.** You shall not at any time prior to the termination of your employment either on your own behalf or for any other person directly or indirectly endeavour to entice away from the Company, any person who is an employee of the Company or otherwise encourage any such employee to breach his contract of employment.

3. **Non-solicitation.** You shall not for a period of . . . . *(insert figure)* months after the termination of your employment either on your own behalf or for any other person directly or indirectly approach, canvass, solicit or otherwise endeavour to entice away from the Company the custom of any person or company who at any time during the . . . . *(insert figure)* months preceding the termination of your employment both has been a customer, client or supplier of the Company and with whom you shall have personally had dealings.

4. **Non-dealing.** You shall not for a period of . . . . *(insert figure)* months after the termination of your employment either on your own behalf or for any other person supply, directly or indirectly and whether solicited by you or not, any goods or services to any person or company who at any time during the . . . . *(insert figure)* months preceding the termination of your employment both has been a customer, client or supplier of the Company and with whom you shall have personally had dealings.

5. **Non-poaching.** You shall not for a period of . . . . *(insert figure)* months after the termination of your employment either on your own behalf or for any other person directly or indirectly approach, canvass, solicit or otherwise endeavour to entice away any person who shall be an employee of the Company at the date of termination of your employment and with whom you had regular contact during the . . . . *(insert figure)* months preceding the termination of your employment with a view to the specific knowledge or skills of such person being used by or for the benefit of any person carrying on business in competition with the business carried on by the Company.

6. **Non-competition.** You shall not for a period of . . . . *(insert figure)* months after the termination of your employment either on your own behalf or on behalf of or in association with any other person directly or indirectly be engaged, concerned or interested as an employee or in any other capacity in any business [within . . . . *(insert figure)* miles radius of . . . . *(insert a specific point)*] [within . . . . *(insert a defined area)*] where you would be acting in direct competition with that part of the business carried on at the date of termination of your employment by the Company with which you were involved as an employee in the . . . . *(insert figure)* months prior to the termination of your employment. That part of the business is defined as . . . . *(insert specific nature of business in which employee was personally involved).*

Always add the following paragraphs to whichever clause you use:

Each sub-clause of this clause constitutes an entirely separate and independent restriction on you. Where any sub-clause of this clause is held void or unlawful or unenforceable in any respect then such sub-clause shall be severed from this contract without prejudice to the validity or enforcement of the other sub-clauses of this contract.

If you should receive from any person, firm or company an offer of employment or engagement to commence at any time during the period of the restrictions set out in this clause, you agree to forthwith provide to such person, firm or company a copy of the restrictions contained in this clause and, if you accept the offer, you shall immediately notify the Company of the person, firm or company's identity and a description of the principal duties of the position accepted and you shall confirm to the Company in writing that you have provided that person, firm or company with a copy of the restrictions contained in this clause.

You acknowledge that you have had the opportunity to take legal advice in relation to the restrictions contained in this clause and agree that, having regard to your particular circumstances, the restrictions contained in this clause are reasonable and necessary to protect the legitimate business interests of the Company.

RETIREMENT POLICY

Retirement age

The Company's policy is to operate a normal retirement age for all employees of .
. . . . *(insert retirement age, normally 65)*. When an
employee reaches this age, their employment will normally come to an end by
reason of retirement.

Alternatively you could have:

The Company does not operate a compulsory normal retirement age. Instead, it
operates a flexible retirement policy that permits employees to choose to retire, or
to be retired by the Company, at any time between the ages of . . . . . *(insert age)*
and . . . . *(insert age)*. Employees should advise their line manager as early as
possible of their wishes in relation to retirement.

The request to continue working beyond retirement procedure

Employees have a statutory right to request to continue working beyond any
retirement age imposed by the Company. The employee's request may be to
continue working either indefinitely, for a specified period or until a specified date.
The Company will give careful consideration to any requests that may be made
by employees to work beyond their intended retirement date, taking into account
the general needs of the business. However, the Company is not obliged to agree
to an employee's request and neither is the Company under any obligation to give
reasons for any refusal to agree to a request.

The Company will notify employees in writing of their intended date of retirement
at least six months, but not more than twelve months, in advance of their intended
retirement date. At the same time, employees will be given details of their right to
request to continue working beyond their intended retirement date.

The following procedure will apply to applications made by employees to work
beyond their intended retirement date:

- employees who wish to submit a request to continue working beyond their
  intended retirement date should do so in writing in accordance with the
  statutory requirements. A form will be provided for this purpose. The form
  should be submitted more than three months, but not more than six months,
  before the intended retirement date notified to the employee by the Company.
  The employee must specify as part of their request whether they would like to
  continue working indefinitely, for a specified period or until a specified date.

The completed form should be submitted to . . . . *(insert name of contact)*

- once a request has been received, the employee will be invited to attend a meeting to discuss their request not to retire on the intended retirement date and to continue working beyond that date

- after the meeting, the employee will be informed in writing of the Company's decision as soon as it is reasonably practicable to do so. If it is decided to continue the employee's employment beyond their intended retirement date, the employee will receive written notification confirming this and reflecting any agreed changes to their contract of employment. If it is decided that the employee will still retire on their intended retirement date, the employee will receive written notification confirming their intended retirement date and informing them of their right to appeal against the decision not to agree to their request to continue working

- employees have the right to appeal against any decision of the Company either not to grant their request to continue working or to grant the request but for a duration which is different from that which the employee actually requested. If the employee lodges an appeal, which they should do as soon as reasonably practicable after receipt of the Company's decision, they will be invited to attend an appeal meeting to discuss their request not to retire on the intended retirement date and to continue working beyond that date

- after the appeal meeting, the employee will be informed in writing of the Company's decision as soon as it is reasonably practicable to do so. The Company's decision on an appeal is final

- employees have the statutory right to be accompanied at the meeting and at any appeal meeting. Their companion may be a work colleague of their choice. Their chosen companion will be permitted to address the meeting and to confer with the employee during the meeting but they will not be permitted to answer questions on the employee's behalf.

SELF-CERTIFICATION OF SICKNESS ABSENCE FORM

This form is to record sickness absence information and is to be completed by you on the first day of return to work and countersigned by your line manager. It must be completed for all periods of sickness absence of half a day or more. If you leave work early on a particular day as a result of sickness, you should record the time you left in the section headed "date on which you first became unfit for work".

If you are absent due to illness for more than seven consecutive calendar days, you must also provide a doctor's certificate.

Once completed, this form will be placed on your personnel file and retained for a period of three years. A separate record will also be kept of your attendance record. The latter will simply record days of sickness absence but will not give the reasons for the absence.

Full name of employee:	
Date on which you first became unfit for work:	
Date on which you returned to work:	
Total number of working days (including half-days) absent due to illness:	
Please give precise details of the nature of your illness or injury - "sick", "ill" or "unwell" is insufficient:	
Did you visit your doctor or seek other medical advice in relation to this period of illness or injury?	YES/NO
If you did not visit your doctor or seek other medical advice, please give the reason why not:	
I declare that the information I have given on this form is true and I confirm that I am now fit to resume work. I understand that it is a serious disciplinary offence to provide false information on this form.	

Name: . . . .   Name: . . . .

(insert name of employee)   *(insert name of line manager)*

Signed: . . . .   Signed: . . . .

Date: . . . .   Date: . . . .

SICKNESS ABSENCE POLICY

Should you be unable to attend work due to illness or injury, you must comply with the following sickness absence reporting procedure:

On the first morning of your sickness absence, you must contact the Company and speak to your line manager at the earliest possible opportunity and as close to your normal start time as possible. In any event, this must be no later than two hours after your normal start time. If you are unable to speak to your line manager personally, you should speak to . . . . *(insert name of contact)*. You should give details of the nature of your illness and, if the illness is of a minor nature, you should indicate when you believe you will be fit to return to work. You must inform your line manager as soon as possible of any change in the date of your anticipated return to work. Contacting your line manager by text message or e-mail is not acceptable, other than in exceptional circumstances. If you have been diagnosed as having contracted an infectious or contagious disease such as measles or chicken pox, or a pandemic virus, you must inform your line manager as soon as possible after your diagnosis.

For an absence of seven consecutive calendar days or less, you are required to telephone your line manager on a daily basis in accordance with the reporting procedure set out above. However, the Company may relax this requirement in exceptional circumstances, for example in the case of a pandemic virus affecting a large percentage of the Company's employees. You will be advised about any modified sickness absence reporting requirements at the appropriate time. You must also complete a self-certification of sickness absence form immediately on your return to work. Self-certification forms are available from (and should be returned once completed to) . . . . *(insert name of contact)*. You are reminded that it is a serious disciplinary offence to provide false information on a self-certification form.

Should your sickness absence be for a period in excess of seven calendar days, you are required as an absolute minimum to contact your line manager on a weekly basis in order to provide an update on your illness or injury. A doctor's certificate must also be obtained. A new doctor's certificate must be submitted each week. Your doctor's certificate must be forwarded to . . . . *(insert name of contact)* as quickly as possible and in any event no later than the end of the calendar week in respect of which the certificate applies.

You should have certificates (either self-certification of sickness absence forms or doctor's certificates) to cover the entire period of your sickness absence.

The Company reserves the right to request a doctor's certificate for any period of sickness absence even though this may be less than eight calendar days. If you incur costs in relation to obtaining a doctor's certificate, the Company will reimburse those costs upon production of a receipt.

Where a doctor's certificate indicates that you may be fit for work and the doctor has suggested ways of helping you get back to work, such as a phased return to work, altered hours, amended duties or workplace adaptations, your line manager will discuss the advice on the doctor's certificate with you and will consider any functional comments made by the doctor, any of the return to work tick boxes and any other action that could help you return to work despite your illness. The various options will be discussed with you and if a return to work is possible, your line manager will agree with you a return to work date, any temporary adaptations or adjustments that are to be made and for how long and will set a date for review. If you disagree with the Company's proposals to support your to return to work, you will be asked to confirm why you believe you cannot return to work despite your doctor's suggestions, and the Company reserves the right to obtain further medical evidence as necessary, such as a medical report. If the Company is not able to make any adaptations or adjustments to help you return to work, your line manager will explain the reasons for this to you and will set a date for review. You may then use the doctor's certificate as if the doctor had advised "not fit for work".

For all periods of sickness absence of half a day or longer, your line manager may require you to attend a "back to work" interview on your return to work to discuss the reasons for your absence and whether it was work-related. In particular, "back to work" interviews will be conducted by line managers each time an employee returns to work following a period of short-term sickness absence of up to one working week. At the interview, you will be advised that your absence record is monitored and recorded in order for the Company to manage performance, identify any problem areas and offer support where appropriate, you will be asked to explain the reasons for your absence and whether you consulted a doctor or attended hospital and you will be requested to complete a self-certification form for the period of your absence. In the case of frequent or repeated absences, your line manager will discuss whether there are any underlying reasons for the regular absences (and, in particular, whether they are in any way work-related) and explore with you whether there is any apparent pattern of absence. You may also be set reasonable targets and time limits for improvement in your attendance and warned that a failure to improve may result in disciplinary action.

For long-term sickness absence, your line manager may request to visit you at home.

For long-term sickness absence or frequent periods of sickness absence, the Company may request a medical report from your GP or consultant or alternatively request that you visit a doctor selected by the Company to undergo a medical examination. The cost of any such report or examination will be met by the Company and you are required to co-operate in the obtaining and disclosure of all results and reports to the Company. The Company will only request you to undergo a medical examination where reasonable to do so.

The Company reserves the right to withhold sick pay in circumstances where the certification procedure described above has not been followed or where there is sufficient reason to doubt the validity of your sickness absence claim. In the latter circumstances, the Company may request you to undergo a medical examination by a doctor selected by it.

On being fit to return to work, you must contact your line manager and let them know as far in advance as possible of the proposed date of your return.

If you have been suffering from an infectious or contagious disease such as measles or chicken pox, or a pandemic virus, you must not report for work until you are medically fit to do so. This is a precautionary measure to prevent the spread of the disease or virus in the workplace.

Persistent short-term sickness absence is, in the absence of any underlying medical condition or other reasonable excuse, a disciplinary matter and will be dealt with in accordance with the Company's disciplinary procedure. If it is subsequently discovered that your sickness absence was not genuine, this will also be treated as a disciplinary matter.

TIME OFF FOR DEPENDANTS POLICY

All employees are entitled to take a reasonable amount of time off during normal hours of work in order to deal with family emergencies. You have no contractual or statutory right to be paid for absences relating to family emergencies. Any payment of salary during time off is made at the absolute discretion of the Company.

The right to take time off enables you to deal with an unexpected or sudden problem and make any necessary longer term arrangements:

- if a dependant falls ill or has been involved in an accident or assaulted

- when your partner is having a baby

- to make longer-term care arrangements for a dependant who is ill or injured to deal with the death of a dependant, for example, making funeral arrangements

- to deal with an unexpected disruption or breakdown in care arrangements for a dependant, for example, when a childminder fails to turn up

- to deal with an incident involving your child whilst they are at school.

For these purposes, a "dependant" is your spouse, partner, child or parent or someone who lives with you as part of your family. It does not include tenants, boarders or employees living in your family home. In cases of illness, injury or where care arrangements break down, a dependant may also be someone who reasonably relies on you for assistance. This may be where you are the primary carer or the only person who can help in an emergency.

In the event of a family emergency occurring while you are at work, you must immediately inform your line manager of the nature of the emergency and seek their express permission to leave work early.

In the event of a family emergency occurring outside your normal hours of work which will prevent you from reporting to work at your normal start time, you must contact the Company and speak to your line manager at the earliest possible opportunity and as close to the normal start time as possible. In any event, this must be no later than two hours after your normal start time. If you are unable to speak to your line manager personally, you should speak to . . . . (*insert name of contact*). You should give details of the nature of the emergency, the reason for your absence and how long you expect to be absent from work. Where the emergency is ongoing, you must report to your line manager on a daily basis and always at least one hour before your normal start time. You must update your line manager on the reason for the ongoing absence and how long you expect it to continue. You must inform your line manager as soon as possible of any change in the date of your anticipated return to work.

The Company envisages that the amount of leave taken will, in most cases, be one or two days at most. The leave to which you are entitled is enough to help you cope with the immediate crisis. You must actively seek alternative longer-term care arrangements for the care of a dependant within one day of the emergency occurring. Should it not be possible to make such arrangements, you must contact your line manager and explain why further absence is required. Authorisation of such continued absence will be at the absolute discretion of your line manager. The right to time off under these rules is intended to cover unforeseen family emergencies. If you know in advance that you are going to need time off, then you should speak to your line manager about the possibility of taking such time as part of your annual leave entitlement.

The Company reserves the right to ask you to provide supporting evidence of the family emergency on your return to work. You must also complete a Family Emergencies Absence Form immediately on your return. These forms are available from . . . . *(insert name of contact)*. You are reminded that it is a serious disciplinary offence to knowingly provide false information on a Family Emergencies Absence Form or to dishonestly claim a right to time off to deal with a family emergency. Any offence will be dealt with in accordance with the Company's disciplinary procedure and, depending on the circumstances, could amount to gross misconduct rendering you liable to summary dismissal.

In the event of a dispute between you and your line manager about whether a particular incident or occurrence falls under the terms of these rules, a Director shall be responsible for determining whether the request for time off made by you relates to a genuine family emergency. Their decision shall be final.

TRAINING AND DEVELOPMENT POLICY

The Company is committed to training and developing all of its employees so as to enable them to achieve their maximum potential. However, it also considers it appropriate to base training and development opportunities on the requirements of the business. Therefore, decisions about investment in staff training and development will always be made having regard to the needs of the business as well as the employee's individual needs.

The Company regularly reviews its level of investment in staff training and development to ensure not only that adequate resources are being provided but also that training and development activity is delivering a benefit to both the employee and the business.

Training and development opportunities

The Company provides a range of training and development opportunities to staff. These include:

- training relating to the enhancement of skills for an employee's current job role. This can include internal and external courses providing technical or specialist training relating to the skills that employees require for their job

- training leading to a professional or academic qualification. The Company encourages employees who wish to do so to pursue continuous professional development and where appropriate to gain further qualifications

- management training, including supervisory skills and leadership development programmes

- health and safety training

- equal opportunities training.

Responsibilities for implementation

Both line managers and employees have a responsibility to implement training and development initiatives. Individual training and development needs and training opportunities will be explored with the employee as part of the performance appraisal process. Line managers should encourage their staff to undertake relevant programmes and employees are expected to take up the opportunities provided and report back to their line manager on their applicability once completed.

Line managers have a responsibility to monitor and evaluate the effectiveness of learning for employees who have undergone training and development, particularly where these have been externally provided. They should consider the quality and cost effectiveness of external training.

Employees should implement the skills that they have gained through training.

New training initiatives

Any new training initiatives will be planned as a result of a training needs analysis during the performance appraisal process. In addition, the Company is committed to reviewing training initiatives so that relevant training and development is provided for skills in specific job areas, where work procedures have changed or where new standards are introduced.

The Company will make use, where appropriate, of e-learning.

Requests for training and development

Employees can request training and development at any time but this will usually be done within the performance appraisal process as outlined above. Employees should make any requests to their line manager. Any decisions on training will be at the absolute discretion of the Company.

Recording of training and development activities

All training attended will be recorded along with costs, including, for example, travel and subsistence expenses and the cost of textbooks.

On completion of any internal or external course the employee may be requested to complete a course evaluation form and return it to either their line manager or the trainer. Analysis of the evaluation forms gathered will be undertaken and used within the overall evaluation of training and development.

Equal opportunities

Decisions relating to training and development will be made fairly and consistently and equality of opportunity will be provided for all staff. Please see the section in this Staff Handbook on Equal Opportunities and Dignity at Work for further information.

WRITTEN STATEMENT OF EMPLOYMENT PARTICULARS

This written statement dated . . . . *(insert date)* meets the requirements of section 1 of the Employment Rights Act 1996 and it supersedes any earlier written or oral arrangement between you and . . . . *(insert name of employer)* ("the Company").

Employee:

. . . . *(insert name of employee)*.

Commencement of employment:

Your employment with the Company commenced on . . . . *(insert date)*. No previous employment counts toward your period of continuous employment with the Company.

Job title:

The title of the job which you are employed to do is . . . . *(insert job title)*. Your duties are those which the Company may from time to time consider as falling within the general ambit of your appointment as . . . . *(insert job title)*. However, the Company may at its discretion amend your duties from time to time, and, in addition to your normal duties you may from time to time be required to undertake additional or other duties as necessary to meet the needs of the business.

Place of work:

Your normal place of work is at . . . . *(insert address)*.

Pay:

Your pay is £ . . . . *(insert figure)* per *(hour / day / week / annum)*. You will be paid . . . . *(insert, e.g., monthly, weekly etc.)* in arrears on or before *the last working day of each (week / month) by direct transfer into your nominated bank or building society account.*

Entirely at the Company's discretion, your pay will be reviewed annually in . . . . . *(insert month)*. The Company is under no obligation to award an increase following a pay review. There will be no review of your pay after notice has been given by either party to terminate your employment.

Hours of work:

Your normal hours of work are . . . . *(insert hours and days, including details of lunch and other breaks)*.

Holidays:

Your annual holiday entitlement is . . . . *(insert number of days)* [inclusive of . . . . *(insert number)* bank and public holidays] and the Company's holiday year runs from . . . . *(insert date)* to . . . . *(insert date)*.

[In addition, you will be entitled to paid annual leave on . . . . *(insert number)* bank and public holidays.]

[As you work part-time, your entitlement to paid annual leave on bank and public holidays is calculated on a pro rata basis according to the days/hours you work. If, due to the particular days of the week that you work, you take more bank and public holidays than your pro rata entitlement, any additional days or part-days taken will be deducted from your annual holiday entitlement. Conversely, if due to the particular days of the week that you work, you take fewer bank and public holidays than your pro rata entitlement, any additional days or part-days will be added to your annual holiday entitlement. This ensures you receive the same number of paid annual leave days overall as full-time employees, calculated on a pro rata basis.]

[However, you may be required to work on bank or public holidays. It is a condition of your employment that you agree to do so when asked by the Company. In this case, the Company will grant you a day off in lieu for each full bank or public holiday worked.]

Additional holiday rules are set out in the Staff Handbook.

Sick pay and reporting sickness absence:

If you are absent from work because of sickness or injury you will be entitled to Statutory Sick Pay, provided you meet the qualifying conditions. Further details about sick pay, and the requirements for reporting sickness absence, are set out in the Staff Handbook.

Pension:

The Company operates a stakeholder pension scheme which you may be entitled to join. Full details of the scheme can be obtained from . . . . *(insert details)*.

Notice:

During the first month of your employment, either the Company or you may give one day's written notice to terminate your employment.

[After one month's continuous service, you are entitled to receive the following written notice of termination of employment from the Company:

More than one month but less than two years' continuous service:	One week
More than two years' continuous service:	One week for each complete year of service up to a maximum of twelve weeks after twelve years' service.

After one month's continuous service, you are required to give the Company one week's written notice of termination of your employment.]

OR

[After one month's continuous service, the Company will give you . . . . . *(insert number)* (weeks'/months') written notice of termination of your employment. Where the statutory minimum notice period is greater than this amount because of your length of service when notice of termination is given, the Company will always ensure you receive at least the statutory minimum notice requirement. After one month's continuous service, you are required to give the Company . . . . . *(insert number)* (weeks'/months') written notice to terminate your employment.]

[If you leave without giving the proper period of notice or you leave during your notice period without permission, the Company shall be entitled, as a result of your agreement to the terms of this [statement/contract], to deduct a day's pay for each day not worked by you during the notice period, provided always that the Company will not deduct a sum in excess of the actual loss suffered by it as a result of your leaving without notice. This deduction may be made from any final payment of salary or other payments or expenses which the Company may be due to make to you. The amount to be deducted is a genuine attempt by the Company to assess its loss as a result of your leaving without giving due notice. It is not intended to act as a penalty upon termination of your employment.]

Disciplinary rules and procedure:

The disciplinary rules and procedure applicable to you are set out in the Disciplinary Procedure section of the Staff Handbook. You are strongly advised to read it.

Appeal procedure:

If you are dissatisfied with any disciplinary decision taken in respect of you, you may appeal to . . . . *(insert details)*. Further details of the appeal procedure are set out in the Disciplinary Procedure section of the Staff Handbook.

Grievance procedure:

The grievance procedure applicable to you is set out in the Staff Handbook.

Collective agreements:

The collective agreements which directly affect your employment are . . . . *(insert details)*.

Acknowledgement:

I acknowledge receipt of this statement. I confirm that I have read the statement and the Staff Handbook which set out the principal rules, policies and procedures relating to my employment.

Signed: . . . .

Print name: . . . .

Dated: . . . .

Notes

Notes

Notes

Notes

Notes

Notes

Notes